THE SUCCESS MODEL

THE SUCCESS MODEL

The Five Step System To Completely

Revolutionize Your Life!

SAM SILVERSTEIN

STAR PUBLISHING™

ST. LOUIS

Publisher's Cataloging in Publication

Silverstein, Sam
    The success model : the five step system to completely
revolutionize your life! / Sam Silverstein
    p.cm.
    Includes index.
    Preassigned LCCN: 93-87199
    ISBN 0-9639-468-4-6

    1. Success   I. Title.

BF637.S8S55 1994   158'.1
                                    QBI93-22330

Printed in the United States of America

Dedication

First and foremost to my wife Renee who provided unending support and endured both my writing and marathon training at the same time. To my children, Geoffrey, Sara, Jaclyn and Allison who, I hope, will some day both understand and apply to their lives, the principles taught in this book. To my grandparents, Celia and Max Wortsman, who showed me by example that you can overcome adversity and achieve in life what you desire. And to my parents, Edith and Rubin, who taught me many valuable lessons - most importantly, if you want something bad enough, you can have it if you are willing to pay the price. I love you all very much.

Acknowledgments

A project of this magnitude and importance would not be possible without the assistance of many special people. It would be difficult to mention every generous person so I would like to thank several groups of people.

My family and friends have been so supportive that it has made this journey an enjoyable one. You have all been an important part of my inner strength. I greatly appreciate the efforts of everyone who reviewed the book, especially my editor Patty Riggins. Thank you for the invaluable feedback. My friends at The National Speakers Association gave so unselfishly of themselves. You are all fantastic. The entire Delsan team has proven that a cohesive unit can overcome any challenge. Your influence has been great. The lessons learned, many.

I would like to extend a special 'Thank you" to Deniz Bilsel. The efforts you put forth on my behalf went beyond that of ordinary friendship. You required much and delivered more. The proof is in the pudding.

Table of Contents

How To Use This Book

Contained in the pages to follow are 57 Key Words and The Success Model. The first five Key Words make up the basis of The Success Model. Be sure you read and fully understand them before proceeding to the chapter on The Success Model. Once you have internalized the first five Key Words and The Success Model, read the other 52 Key Words. Each Key Word is presented in its own short chapter. The chapters have been designed to be to the point and fast paced. All the Key Words relate directly to one or more parts of The Success Model. Internalizing all the Key Words will help round out your understanding of success. As you read, I challenge you to ask the question, "How can I apply this concept to my life?"

I have found that successful people have a certain "air" about them. They not only understand but also project and live the principles taught in this book. It is my hope that you, too, will have this special inner feeling when you fully comprehend, internalize, and apply the philosophy that follows.

Life Is Good;
You Can Make It Better

All people are born with the latent ability to be successful. We must learn and apply the skills that will bring out the success inherent in each of us. Life should not be a compromise. You have the right to accomplish everything in life that you want. The major objective of this book is to teach the techniques and help you apply the proven methodology necessary to be successful in all the endeavors of your life.

The same techniques that worked to achieve success in the 1700's worked in the 1800's, worked again in the 1900's and will also work in the 21st century. These are the techniques I have used and are the basis of The Success Model. The Success Model will enable you to determine exactly what it is that you want in life and help you achieve it. Since you cannot hit a target you don't know is there, it is important to know what it is that you are aiming for. Once you know what it is you really want, you can then apply the rest of The Success Model to achieve your success.

To be able to fully implement The Success Model in

your life, you will need to know all the factors that will influence the outcome of your efforts. I refer to these factors as *Key Words*. I believe that there are a few key words that, when correctly understood and properly applied, will lead you to ultimate success. Words are extremely powerful. They can create. They can destroy. Understanding the key words to success is critical. The right words can lead to riches (not necessarily defined in terms of money); the wrong words can lead to mediocrity or failure. The right words, at the right time, might help you close a sale. The wrong words could blow it. The words "I love you" can seal a wonderful, long-lasting relationship. Just as you must choose the right words when speaking with others, you must choose the right words when speaking to yourself. Understanding and implementing the right words is building the foundation for a life filled with achievement.

You are remembered by your achievements, not by the tasks you don't undertake. Your ability to achieve is limited only by your vision and imagination. Your in-born success mechanism will allow you to accomplish anything you set out to do. The goal of the entire process is to enable you to live a happier, more fulfilled, satisfied life and to help you maintain that state through time; day in and day out, year in and year out. Your on-going daily achievement will provide you continued satisfaction and happiness.

One summer while in college, I sold athletic shoes for a department store in Atlanta. My department was separate from the other shoe departments and my immediate supervisor worked upstairs in the ladies shoe department. Being a runner, I had a high interest in athletic shoes and I poured my energy and enthusiasm into my job. I always made sure that my customers were fit with the right shoe for their needs. One time I even delivered a pair of shoes to an elderly woman's home because she couldn't get out. When the time came for a performance review, the department head came down and showed me a standard evaluation form. On it he graded me as average in every category and gave me a $.05 an hour raise. Now, I knew I wasn't perfect, but I sincerely felt that I was above average in many categories, certainly at least one or two. I was insulted and hurt and decided right then I would not leave my life in anybody else's hands. I would take control of my own destiny. In the future, I would only take a sales position where I earned a commission. I knew that I could control my earnings through my skills and my efforts.

Take control of *your* future. *Your* successes are in *your* hands. Commit to change. Set your goals. Apply the principles taught in this book. The process is simple; it is the application that takes supreme effort and commitment. You can't do it, you say? Of course you can. Thousands of others have done it. You say they were lucky? (see Luck.) You think they are different? Well, even our forefathers over 200 years ago knew something that you must accept: "all men are created equal." Of course, I would add women to that. You see, it is not the past that will determine your future, it is the present. For example, with respect to financial success, any past failures will not determine your future. It is not uncommon for very successful people to have failures in their past. Donald Trump has made millions, lost millions and made millions again.

Even education is not a guarantee of financial success. There are people all over the world that have achieved a high level of financial success with limited formal education. Levi Strauss never completed high school. He built the largest clothing company in the world. Edwin Land dropped out of college. He went on to be the founder of Polaroid. What you do *now* will decide your level of achievement in the future. Do not let your perception of the past affect your perception of the future. Your slate is clean. Fill your slate with the knowledge you gain from this book and apply it in your life.

I am a partner in a window manufacturing business. At one time, we were having production problems. We had trouble delivering windows on a timely basis and maintaining quality. I realized then that the solutions to our manufacturing problems were easy to develop, but applying those solutions to get the desired results was difficult. The same applies to the process for success in your life. The system is simple. Applying the system to your life will take effort.

You will have challenges.
You can overcome.
You will face brick walls.
You can break through.
You will encounter doubters.
You will persevere.

Some people are happy with beans for dinner, some want steak. It's okay to eat beans if that is what you truly want. Some people simply choose the status quo. They are happy with what they have and choose not to put forth the effort. For them, this is fine. Is it fine for you? *You* must decide what makes you happy. *You* must decide what it is you want out of life. Calculate what the price will be to get what you want, and then pay it. Achievement doesn't happen by accident, but total fulfillment can be yours.

To have a more successful and fulfilled life you need two things:

Knowledge & Application

Knowledge is learning the techniques necessary to successfully achieve the goals you set for yourself.

Application is actually using those techniques to get your positive results.

Someone once said, "It's not what you know that counts, it's who you know." I believe "it's not *just* what you know, it's how you use what you know that will determine your ultimate outcome." It would be one thing not to know how to be more successful. I feel it a real crime when someone knows the techniques but, through procrastination or neglect, never applies the methodology and remains "average." If you learn the concepts, the techniques, and the philosophies taught in this book and apply them to your life, the most remarkable and rewarding success will be yours.

Study the key words. Internalize them until they become yours. Understand how their definitions affect The Success Model and apply the model to your life. You can start achieving and increase your success today!

Desire

All human activity is prompted by desire.
- Bertrand Russell -English mathematician and philosopher.

Desire is the first step of The Success Model. The power necessary to accomplish in life what you want to accomplish comes from within and is generated by your primary desires. Your "success energy" is derived from your primary desires. It is this success energy that translates into the commitment and enthusiasm needed to follow through on your plans. The key to desire is that it must be internalized. Desire must come from within and flow from the inside out. Therefore, outside stimuli, such as myself, will not sustain *your* desire. I can only teach you how to create the desire from within, and only then will you be able to sustain it because the desire is genuine.

To begin any journey towards achievement one must start with desire. Desire is the beginning of all greatness. Desire must burn within you. Lee Iacocca was fired by Ford, but his desire brought him back and he has been credited with saving Chrysler Corporation. Abraham Lincoln lost six elections and nominations, including those for the state legislature, U.S. Senate, and U.S. House of Representatives, before winning and becoming the President of the United States. The goal you desire must be so important that you will use all your skills and develop new ones, if necessary, to achieve success.

When you were little, there was something that you really wanted. Maybe it was a bicycle or other toy. You asked and asked your parents until you finally got it. The reason you worked so hard on your parents was because they held the key to get what it was that you wanted. Now, *you* hold the key to whatever it is you want. The key is what we call "primary desire." You must work on yourself now just as hard as you worked on your parents then!

Most people know what they don't want and not what they do want. To better understand what it is that qualifies as our primary desires, let's consider the following situation. My driveway is 100 feet long. You are at one end of my driveway and I am standing at the other end. I have a $100.00 bill in my hand and offer it to you if you will walk down my driveway and get it. Will you? Most people would. Now, consider the following. I have covered my driveway with a bed of hot coals. The coals cover the driveway from end to end and side to side. Will you walk through the fire hot coals for the $100.00? My guess is no. Now, I'm going to take your shoes and socks away so you are completely barefoot. There is a fence lining each side of my driveway. The fire hot coals are 12 inches deep. I am holding a bag with one-hundred-thousand-dollars in it. Will you walk down my driveway for the money. My guess is still no. I have placed a dozen 5-gallon cans of gasoline at various places along the driveway. Taped to the sides of the cans are several sticks of dynamite. There is a fan blowing on the coals and they are really heating up. Flames are starting to lick up around the gas cans. There will be an explosion at any moment. To sweeten the deal, I am holding a briefcase with one million dollars in it. Would you walk through the fire hot coals? My guess is that the answer is still "no." Let's make one last change to this scenario. I am holding your daughter (son, mother, father, or other family member) over one of the cans of gasoline and the temperature is rising very rapidly. Now, will you walk down the driveway?

The bottom line is: what are you willing to "walk through fire" for? The answer to this question is the basis for your primary desires. Of course, I am not suggesting that you will have to walk through fire. What I am saying is that for a desire to be a primary desire it must be intense. Throughout this book I will refer back to the analogy of "walking through fire." When I do, I am referring to an extremely intense desire. This is an "absolutely-have-to-have-it" attitude.

Once you know what is important in your life and what you stand for, your primary desires will evolve into short and long-term goals. What are *your* primary desires? It is necessary to list, define, and prioritize your primary desires before you can begin the journey toward personal success. You must know what it is you believe in and stand for. What is it that is truly important to you? It is your primary desires for which you will set goals. These are the areas in which you want to achieve specific positive results. For your goals to be great enough to affect change in your habits, your goals must be based on your primary desires.

These are the only desires strong enough to create long-term motivation.

Take a piece of paper and list your primary desires. Don't limit yourself. If it is really important, put it down. Make sure they are desires for which you are willing to "walk through fire". Don't worry that what you want to do in life may not pay enough or that you don't know how to go about achieving what it is you want. If you really want it, put it down. You will be able to figure out how to get your desires and how to have exactly what it is you want. Let's say you want to teach and help people improve their lives. You are thinking that an elementary teacher's salary won't allow you to fulfill your financial primary desires. What about seminars? Maybe teaching in large groups would pay better. Some "teachers" work with corporations and organizations. The fees that are associated with this type of teaching can be quite substantial. So you see, you can teach *and* reach your financial primary desires!

If you have "wants" that are not primary desires, your energy and commitment will not carry you through to completion. A friend of mine has a wonderful wood shop in his basement. He has a 20-foot bench with electric outlets every three feet. On the bench are several pieces of equipment. He has an electric sander, a drill press, a jig saw, a table saw and more. My son is a Cub Scout. The scouts race pine wood cars that the children make. Each year when it is time for my son to make his pine wood derby car, we go down the street and use the shop in my friend's basement. Each year I think that I would like my own wood shop. I say that I will go out and buy the equipment and build a shop in my basement. Several years have come and gone and I still haven't gone out to buy the tools and machines. The reason is, although a wood shop seems nice, it really isn't a primary desire of mine to have one. If you are not willing to "walk through fire for" an item, strike it out, remove it from your list. Don't look at items that aren't primary desires. Don't think about them. They will just get in your way. If they are not primary desires, you won't have the enthusiasm and passion for them anyway. If they are not primary desires, you don't need them on your list. If they are primary desires, you want them on your list because you are going to work for and achieve them.

Now, define in as much detail as possible what each of these primary desires mean to you. What is a good job? How much money do you want to earn? What specific net worth do you want and by when do you want to accomplish it? What type of hours are you willing to work? With what type of people do you want to associate? Be specific! By knowing exactly what it is you desire you will know exactly what to work towards and you will know when you attain it.

Then, prioritize your primary desires. What is most important, second, third and so on. Remember that, although you are prioritizing these desires, there may be times in your life when your priorities will change for a while. This is okay .

Be sure that your desires don't conflict with one another. It would be difficult to work the 70-80 hours necessary to start a new business while at the same time lifting weights one-and-one-half hours a day, reading four books a week, donating seven hours weekly to your religious affiliation and having time for an enriched family life and social development. When your desires clash, frustration rises. Frustration is a de-motivator and should be eliminated. You can't completely dedicate yourself to a business venture 70-80 hours a week, and exercise, and read more books, and spend more time with the children. There are only so many hours in the day. Remember, at some period in your life, some primary desires may have to take a back seat to others. You should constantly review your primary desires and your priorities (see Balance).

An important characteristic about your primary desires is their strength. Your primary desires will motivate you to the point that nothing will stand in your way of achieving exactly what it is you want. If you *knew* that you could indeed achieve your goals and that it is not a matter of *if*, but *when*, then when would you begin working on your goals? (*How* is not important because we will discuss that later.) You would begin right now, wouldn't you?! Well, the fact is, if you define your primary desires and run them through The Success Model, you will be successful.

In June of 1993 Sergi Bruguera of Spain won the French Open. In doing so Bruguera, twenty-two, beat the two time reigning champion Jim Courier in the final match. At the trophy presentation ceremony Bruguera told the cheering crowd; "I'll tell you a secret - ever since I was six years old, my birthday wish was to win the French Open." That is an intense primary desire.

Your primary desire will create so much force that you will have to succeed. I once heard an analogy of opportunity knocking. Opportunity doesn't knock, you will knock. Your primary desires will force you to knock so hard you will knock the door down. You will pick the lock if that is what it takes to get what you want. The power that your primary desires generate is that strong.

You will find that just the exercise of listing and defining your primary desires will add more meaning and direction to your life. You have now laid the corner stone necessary to apply The Success Model to your life.

Change

Keep changing. When you're through changing, you're through.
- Francis Bacon -Seventeenth century English philosopher and essayist.

> **Change is the essence of progress.**

If change is the essence of progress, then we cannot have any improvement unless we are willing to commit to change. Change, which is the second step in The Success Model, can only be initiated as the result of a primary desire. Lasting change is possible only when the need and desire for change is both understood and internalized. People will not change until they are ready to change. No one can force you to change. No one can start the process of change for you, except yourself. As human beings, we have the ability to change any thing and any time we want. Are *you* ready to change?

Many people are "too comfortable" to initiate change. They are too comfortable to risk failure. If we do today what we did yesterday, we will get the same results tomorrow that we are getting today, or worse. ***To achieve any level of meaningful improvement we must consider and implement change.*** In business, if you don't improve, you will move back, because your competition will improve and pass you by.

Let's say you want to lose weight. There are two variables that you can control, what you eat and how much you exercise. If you eat the same way today as you always have, and you don't change your exercise habits, your weight won't change. Now, let's say you change the food you eat so that you are reducing fat and calories. Even if you don't change your exercise routine, the change in food intake alone will change your weight situation. Likewise if you don't change your eating habits but increase your exercise regime, you will burn more fuel and lose weight. Of course, the best thing to do would be to modify your intake and increase your outflow through a good exercise program. To maximize my performance as a runner I needed to lose some weight. I went on a low fat diet. Less than 25% of my calories were from fat. I also increased the frequency and length of my running workouts. As a result I lost 14 pounds!

It's common and expected that people will try to stay in their comfort zone. This is an area where risk is minimal. Chances are not taken. Failure is not a consideration. This is where we're "comfortable" and where we know we can "handle" almost any situation that comes up. Greatness does not exist in the comfort zone. The comfort zone is for people who are not looking to better their position in any of the seven major areas of life (see Balance). To succeed in life one must recognize that "trips" out of the comfort zone are not only necessary but also required. Most people are afraid of change. However, it's only through change that we can improve.

As the illustration below shows, there are more opportunities (O) outside the comfort zone than there are inside.

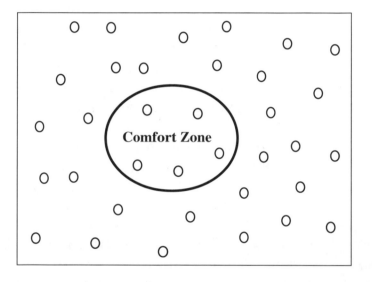

The space inside your comfort zone is finite, it is limited. The area outside the comfort zone is infinite, it has no limits.

For example, if a runner can run a mile in seven minutes and always trains in his comfort zone, he will always run a 7-minute mile. Maybe he is happy with his time. If so, that is okay. All of his workouts will be similar, non-taxing, and he won't test his ability. However, if he wants to improve, he must not only desire the improvement, but also be willing to leave his comfort zone so he can achieve long term success in running (his chosen area of desired success). By adding more difficult workouts to his training regime that push his limits, tax his respiratory system, jack up his heart rate, and increase the lactic acid in his bloodstream, he can improve and grow as a runner. His threshold will be raised and his time lowered. The change in the workouts may be somewhat uncomfortable or even downright difficult, but it is obligatory to improving performance and lowering times, which is the goal he established from his primary desires. The satisfaction of achieving his primary desire will be greater and last longer than the pain (price paid) he endured to achieve his primary desire.

The difference between the animals and human beings is that people have the ability to change. We can change our lives. We can change our surroundings. We can change our habits. We can change our future based on changes we make today! The salmon swim upstream every year at the same time. The swallows arrive at Capistrano every year at the same time. Grizzly bears crawl into their caves every year at the same time. But if you're tired of your job, if you're tired of your attitude, if you're tired of your relationships, if you're tired of your physique: if you want something better, you have the power to change and get what you want out of life. Human beings have the ability to change and to shape what they become.

Ask yourself the following questions:

Have you fulfilled *all* of your primary desires?

Is the comfort level of what you have now more important than the unknown of working toward your goals?

Will you be happy later in life if you haven't put forth your best efforts to achieve your dreams?

If the answer to any of these questions is "no," or you are unsure, then you should move forward by initiating change. Only through change can you break existing patterns and start new ones. By changing how you think and act, you can change your results. Accept the philosophy of change. The methodology for achieving change is discussed in the chapter on habits. Apply this system to your life, then go through the steps in The Success Model. By making changes in your attitudes and habits you will actually have a paradigm shift (see Paradigm). You will be able to incorporate concepts and tasks into your plan that, before, you would have thought impossible.

If you have limited thinking, you will have limited plans. Change involves an expansion in thinking. A commitment to change means opening your mind, realizing the need to make improvements in your personal habits and behaviors and being able to consider new concepts so that you can have the creative plans necessary to achieve your primary desires. Make a personal commitment to change and growth will follow.

Plan

Successful generals make plans to fit circumstances, but do not try to create circumstances to fit plans.
- General George S. Patton, Jr -United States Army, World War II.

     The third step in The Success Model is the plan. The plan is a step-by-step program for reaching your goals. Critical attention must be given to this step-by-step approach. The key to the plan is making each concept work on paper *before* you try to make it work in the real world.

     For example, if you were going to a bank to borrow money to start up a company, the loan officer would want to see a detailed business plan. In your presentation you would need to provide at least the following:

- A description of your product or service.
- An explanation of your potential customer base.
- Information about where your business would be located, including demographics of the area.
- Projected financial statements for the first few years of operation. These should include information pertaining to lease expenses, employee compensation,

utilities, fix-up expenses, inventory, equipment, supplies, etc.
- A cash flow projection to make sure that cash on hand would be sufficient to handle the peak periods of business.
- A list of potential suppliers.
- The suppliers terms and any "exclusives" or protected territories.
- A personal biography listing your experience and qualifications.

As you can see, the bank would want to see in great detail what it is you are attempting to do. The loan officer would then decide, among other things, whether your business plan made sense on paper.

Treat all of your goals the same way. If you put down on paper, in great detail, how you plan to go about achieving your goals, then you will have a map to follow along your journey.

If you lived in New York and decided to go to Miami for a vacation, would you just load up the car and drive off? How about a map? Which roads are you going to take? If you just drive, you could end up in Chicago instead of Miami. However, if you have a map and follow a pre-determined route, drive at a steady speed, take planned breaks, and spend the night at pre-determined motels, what are the chances that you would arrive relatively close to the time you project? Pretty good, don't you think? If you would do that for your vacation, why not do that for the primary desires in your life?!

Some people like to "wing it," thinking that challenges will just take care of themselves. Much time is wasted making decisions along the way that should have been anticipated and addressed in advance. This approach can result in many wrong turns, costing both time and money. A good detailed map would get them to their destination on time.

Even something fun and recreational like snow skiing requires that you map out your moves. The goal in skiing is to enjoy both the pleasure of the outdoors and the exhilaration of skiing down a mountain while keeping all your body parts intact. You put your skis on and ride a lift to the top of the mountain. That is the time to prepare your journey down the mountain, keeping in mind your goal (of reaching the bottom in one piece). The one thing that skiers should do, either on the ride up the mountain or after unloading from the ski lift, is check their trail map. Beginner and intermediate skiers prefer to ski the easier trails. They are shown on the map. The advanced skier, however, uses his trail map to successfully navigate all of the trails. The trail map is the plan a skier uses to go where he wants and to stay "in bounds," so that he doesn't ski out of safe areas and off a cliff.

The quality of your plan will directly relate to your level of success. **There are three major steps involved in creating your plan.**

1. Research
2. Write
3. Review

The first step in the plan is to find out what the *price* is to achieve your primary desire. What education is required? What habits will you need to enhance, or change or acquire? How much time is involved? How much start-up capital will you need? What contacts need to be made? The necessary research should be done before writing the plan. Allocate 60% of the time you will be spending on your plan to research. By doing thorough and detailed research, you will be able to write a better plan, the one best suited to help you obtain the desired results. When you begin your project, be as prepared as you possibly can, since you can expect some surprises along the way.

Your plan must be written. A written plan gives you definite steps to follow. By writing down your plan, you will reinforce your commitment to the project. A detailed plan should have daily, weekly, monthly, and even yearly goals. All segments of the plan should have a time frame or deadlines for completion. Deadlines pull you through your plan and help you resist procrastination. Contingencies for items such as potential problems and necessary continuing education should be built into the plan. The more detailed and better defined the plan the easier it will be to follow and to accurately gauge your progress. The writing phase of developing your plan is in effect a boiling down of the infor-mation you uncovered during research. This phase should comprise 30% of the time you put into your plan.

Before giving your plan the final seal of approval, review it. Seek out an expert or mentor (see Mentor). Others may be able to review your plan without the emotion that you carry. Successful people are usually willing to help and give advice. Use feedback from them to readjust your plan into its final version. You should allocate 10% of the total time spent on your plan for reviewing and fine tuning the plan.

Begin today by writing your plan. When it is completed, start *at once* with the first phase. There is no time like *today* to start down the road to success.

Implementation

Few men are lacking in capacity, but they fail because they are lacking in application.
- Calvin Coolidge -Thirtieth President of the United States.

Implementation is the fourth step in The Success Model. Implementation is what separates the winners from the losers. Implementation is what distinguishes the real super achievers from others. If you don't implement the truths, the system, the plan that works, how can you possibly achieve?!

Good implementation is the result of three major factors:

1. Developing a quality, realistic plan.
2. Knowing and sticking to objectives.
3. Evaluating progress and making changes when necessary.

A good plan will lend itself to successful implementation. Conversely, a bad plan will be difficult, if not impossible, to implement.

If you won't settle for less than great effort, you won't have to live with less than great results. You must outline and know your objectives each step of the way. Then, you must stick to those objectives. Too often, people get bogged down in mundane tasks and unimportant issues. Manage your time wisely. By sticking to objectives, you will be concentrating on those areas that will produce the results necessary to accomplish each step of your plan and lead to your ultimate success (see Focus).

Part of implementation is evaluating your progress. Your plan should include built-in "mini" goals or check points. If you are accomplishing your mini goals, then you will reach your major goal. But if you are straying off course, you must make changes along the way. Making adaptations is normal and healthy. By making corrections, you will continually move towards your ultimate goal.

Dr. Edward Deming, a world renowned manufacturing management and quality expert who has been credited with inspiring and shaping the highly successful Japanese manufacturing system, teaches a total quality manufacturing management system with the acronym **PDCA** (plan, do, check, act). We already know that the third step in The Success Model is the plan. Implementation, would be similar to the "do," "check," and "act" facets of Deming's PDCA philosophy. Once the plan is created, it is time to start implementation.

When a captain gets ready to leave port he picks his destination (a goal derived from a primary desire). Then, with nautical charts in hand, he maps out a course (plan). As he sails along (implementation), he knows that the tides and winds affect his ship, moving him off course. So from time to time, he sights the stars or uses satellites for position readings to determine exactly where he is at any given moment (evaluate). If he is off course a little, he makes the necessary adjustments to get back on course (change). Over the entire journey he may make several such adjustments, until he eventually reaches his destination. This process is the same in your life. Your desire must push you to write out your goal and proceed on your journey.

The value of the journey is greater than the value of any single goal. Once the methodology of success is learned, internalized, and implemented you will be able to move through life achieving one goal after another. During the process of attaining your goals, you will learn a great deal about yourself and the world around you. It is this knowledge that you will continuously build upon and use for future goal-setting and achieving.

Success

I want to be all that I am capable of becoming.
- Katherine Mansfield -Twentieth century British writer.

Success, the fifth step in The Success Model, is the positive results received from your daily achievements in pursuit of your primary desires. The reason that this definition of success works is because it applies to everyone. However, not all people are the same. A person's uniqueness is expressed in their primary desires and the goals they set for *themselves*. In other words, one person's primary desires and goals may be completely different from another person's. They are both achieving success through the achievement of their own primary desires.

Results are the natural conclusion of the first four steps in The Success Model. What this means is that you only have to concentrate on 80% of The Success Model. If you properly apply the first four steps, in your life, the last step, success, will take care of itself. You can now afford to spend 100% of your time, energy, enthusiasm, and effort on steps One through Four. If you do a good job, your desired results will be automatic!

How do you know when you are successful? (Success in not measured only in monetary terms.) What's important in life is achieving success in all areas. Balance is essential. Success is measured in the *accomplishment* of your primary desires. Your primary desires and resulting goals may include health and family, social, educational, recreational and spiritual areas as well. Success is an everyday lifestyle (see Balance).

If you are not striving to excel, you will automatically be attracted to mediocrity. Success is not only knowing the principles, but also falling in love with the concepts of achievement. Become enthusiastic about the subject of success and study it as if it was your favorite hobby. If you treat success as a hobby (research it, learn its techniques, apply your skill), you will enjoy the daily process (as well as the results) of success.

Human beings have a common denominator. We have a right to succeed. We are all born with tools that allow us to set goals and work toward these goals. You must tap these inner abilities and qualities. Do this by practicing. Set and achieve smaller goals before you move on to bigger and more challenging ones. This is all part of mastering these important techniques. All people desire and all people can have success. It is just that success will be different for each individual.

You must have a personal commitment in order to move forward on your goals. Higher and higher goals are attainable by continuing to stretch your level of ability. Just as an athlete reaches a new best time, or height, or other milestone, just as athletes break through barriers and move on to new and greater personal records, we as individuals must stretch our limits. We must increase our capabilities and always continue to grow. If we reach one goal and then don't set a new goal, we will soon become complacent. Continued growth is necessary to maintain a feeling of self-satisfaction.

The beauty is that you can have immediate gratification by enjoying the process of attaining your goals. When you are working on one of your primary desires, your high energy will create enjoyment each step of the way. You will actually be able to enjoy the results *before* you achieve them! Even as I write this book I have the satisfaction and enjoyment of working on one of my primary desires. I enjoy the time I spend and the knowledge I gain. Each time I sit in front of my computer, I get excited about writing and about the progress I am making. I don't look at the process as a chore but rather as the pursuit of my dream and the fulfillment of my goals. Writing this book is one of my primary desires. This book enables me to share with and teach others the techniques I used to achieve success. It also gives me the opportunity to have a positive impact on others lives.

Let's take this concept one step further. As I write this book, I am also training for the Boston Marathon. Each day I train with immense enthusiasm. Each day I am achieving and progressing in my training. I can see increases in both speed and endurance. Surely, I am able to enjoy now my primary desires for fitness even as I am working for a *future* event. My primary desire is to maintain an excellent level of personal fitness, a level that will allow me the opportunity to participate in most any activity I desire as I grow older. My recreational desire is to compete in the

Boston Marathon, the only race other then the Olympic trials in which a runner must qualify by running a specific time in a prior, sanctioned race. For the Gods of running, Boston is their heaven.

Going even further, tonight I played with my children, read them books and said prayers together before tucking them into bed. These activities give me great satisfaction and accomplishment with respect to my primary desire of being a good father.

The point I am making is that you can enjoy success in all the important areas of life *now*. You are not limited to having success in only one area at a time and you don't have to sacrifice present gratification for future gratification. Think about it. You can have everything you want now and not have to wait until some unknown time in the future. It's the tremendous enthusiasm that accompanies your primary desires that gives you the immediate satisfaction of daily achievement toward the eventual completion of your long-term goals.

THE SUCCESS MODEL

Desire accomplished is sweet to the soul.
- Old Testament: Proverbs, xiii, 19.

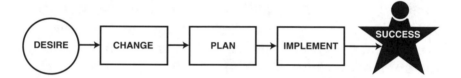

Most people go through life only dreaming of things they would like to achieve. Successful people are those who know how to minimize the difference between their dreams and reality. The Success Model can help you shrink the gap between *your* dreams and *your* reality.

The magnitude of your results will be in direct proportion to the intensity applied to each part of the model. How strong is your desire? How great is your willingness to change? How detailed are your plans? How committed are you to the implementation of your plans? The level of passion applied to each segment will determine the effectiveness of your results and the amplitude of your success.

One of the most fascinating facts about The Success Model is that you have to be concerned with just four of the five parts, which is just 80% of the model. You will be able to apply 100% of your time, energy, and effort to only four steps. The fifth step, the other 20%, will automatically take care of itself! If you clearly figure out what it is you want (primary desires), commit to change, research and write a great plan, and then with enthusiasm, commitment, and energy implement the plan while overcoming crises along the way, the success part of the model will be realized automatically. Remember our definition of results? ***Results are the natural conclusion of the first four steps in The Success Model.*** In this case results is success.

Let's run an example through The Success Model. Your primary desire is:

"I want to start my own company and build it to a level of success such that I will be able to earn a minimum of $200,000.00 annually."

Now, to run the desire through The Success Model, we will make the following assumptions:

- You are currently employed by another company.
- You have very little money saved.
- The business you want to start is in another field than you are currently working in.

Sounds like a tough situation, but let's see how the process works.

For The Success Model to work, the above stated

desire must be a *primary* desire. You must be willing to "walk through fire" for it. If this is sincerely the case, the next step is Change.

Change is necessary to shift from your present course to the new course aimed at achieving your primary desire. You must accept the challenge of your primary desire. You will need to mentally (and sometimes physically) commit to the concept of change. All changes must be aimed at improvements and enhancements in your habits and skills. These changes will allow you to accept new responsibilities, duties and perform the tasks necessary in the implementation stage of The Success Model. Maybe you will have to start work at 6:00 A.M. instead of 8:00 A.M. each day. It is possible you will have to improve your communication skills or possibly learn some accounting. Sales skills may need polishing. These are just a few areas to think about.

Your planning stage will require research before the detailed writing begins. Ask yourself the following questions:

What industry will your company be in?
Who will be your competition?
What is the growth potential in this industry?
Who can I talk with to get valuable information about the industry?
Who can I talk with to get valuable information about business in general?
How much capital is involved in a start-up?
What else do I need to know about starting and running this business?

The research phase should be thorough. Write your plan based on the information you gather. Review your plan with a *qualified* person. A qualified person is someone who has education or experience in something similar to what you are planning. A twelve-year-old may be able to give good, practical advice on rollerblading, but a child would be a terrible source for marriage counseling. I stress the word "qualified" because sometimes people mistakenly ask family members to review plans. Although chosen family members may have good intentions, they may not have the appropriate business experience in this case to provide quality feedback. Finally, when the plan is in its completed form, begin to implement it *at once*!

Let's look at a possible challenge in your plan. Based on the amount of money needed to start, you will have to determine whether or not you can earn it in your current job. Let's say that the company you want to start requires $5,000.00. If you won't be able to save it out of your current paycheck, can you borrow this money from someone else? If not, then let's look at a second job. If you work a second job for 15 hours a week and clear $6.50 an hour you will have your $5,000.00 in less than a year. You might ask yourself, "Do I want to work a second job?" If so, then also ask if this is a primary desire. Are you willing to "walk through fire" to achieve success? How bad do you want it? During the first year of your plan, while earning the $5,000.00 required, continue to research and make additional contacts. Adjust your plan as you refine the information gathered.

If your plan is based on sound research and realistic expectations, you will be able to implement it according to your time schedule. It may take six months. It may take six years, but you will be able to accomplish the goals you set out to achieve, those based on your primary desires. You will need energy, enthusiasm, and commitment among other skills to successfully implement your plan. A friend of mine went from earning $5.50 an hour to over $400,000.00 a year in less than seven years by using this method!

My wife, Renee, had high cholesterol. She knew that her good health depended on bringing down her cholesterol. She has a primary desire to be healthy. Renee knew that she would have to make dietary changes and changes in her exercise program. After consulting with her doctor, Renee put together a plan comprised of two major parts. The first part outlined the type and frequency of workouts. She exercised five to six times a week. Both tennis and strenuous walking were part of the program. Simultaneously, she read books on diet and low-fat cooking. Everyone's eating habits in the Silverstein household changed and we all reduced the fat in our diets. The results? Renee's high cholesterol of 238 was reduced to 154. Renee, her doctor, and I were pleased with the results. Renee had a well-defined goal based on her primary desire. She committed to change, researched and wrote a good plan. Then, she implemented the plan by modifying her cooking habits and changing her schedule to fit in more exercise. Every morning she walked on the treadmill. She played tennis. Most dinners became an adventure in new recipes. The results took care of themselves.

Let's say you have a primary desire of having the best possible family life. You have defined in detail that a great family life is comprised of an outstanding relationship with your wife as well as a closeness and sharing with well behaved children. You commit to change in your time allocations and some personal habits. The plan you write is based on research done:

1) Reading well accepted books on parenting and personal relationships.

2) Interviewing other couples who have well behaved children.

3) Attending seminars on marriage and parenthood.

You and your wife agree to write out a plan *together*. This plan would detail how you are going to raise your children, what types of values you want to instill in them, your discipline style and your reward system. Your plan would also detail items pertaining to your relationship with your spouse. Maybe part of the plan is a yearly trip, just the two of you. Begin implementing that plan. Since long-term relationships are based on long-term efforts, success is enjoyed and implementation is continued. The family and marriage you always wanted can be yours!

My window company had a long-term reputation for quality and service. Over a period of two to three years, our traditional good performance started to slide. Lead times extended out to six weeks. Our competition seized the opportunity and offered a guaranteed two-week delivery program. We called a meeting of sales, manufacturing, and front office personnel. We decided then that we wanted a total manufacturing program that would enable us to offer one-week turnaround on orders. This meant that changes would have to be made in credit approval procedures so that orders would not be delayed. We also realized that changes would have to be made in order entry and scheduling, as well as manufacturing. A plan was put together by our Director of Operations, reviewed, and then re-submitted with substantial changes. The revised plan was implemented, and within three weeks our turnaround time fell to the desired one-week goal. The best part was that our manufacturing costs also dropped. This resulted in an annual cost savings of over $250,000.00!

An associate of mine was having trouble just getting through the day. She was in poor physical shape and just finishing the workday took extreme effort. Rose, realized that in order to enjoy all life had to offer it was imperative to get into good condition. Being in top physical shape became a primary desire for Rose. Rose, made two major changes in her life; she went on a low fat diet and she committed to an exercise program. Rose had a goal of entering and completing a road race within two months. She also wanted to fit into a specific dress for her son's wedding that was in four months. The dress was four sizes smaller than the size she was currently wearing. Rose outlined what would be and would not be in her new diet. She then committed to the philosophy of "being in training." This diet and training plan is what she would implement in the days to come. The first day Rose went for a walk it was physically all she could do to walk one and one-half miles. When she got home from her walk Rose collapsed on the couch. Slowly and persistently Rose extended the length of her workouts and the pace she did them in. Within 60 days Rose entered and completed a 7.2 mile road race and within three and one-half months had lost over thirty pounds! For her son's wedding Rose fit into the dress she had bought four months prior.

Rose told me, "Exercise used to be such a chore. I hated it. Now I enjoy exercise. For the past four months I have been able to enjoy, on a daily basis, the impending success of reaching my health goals." Rose was able to attain her primary desire of improved health. Today she exhibits an over-abundance of energy and an improved zest for life. On top of it all she looks great!

Success is not usually easy to achieve, but it is very possible and definitely wonderful once you have it. The painstaking efforts you make will be long forgotten as you enjoy the rewards of your success.

Read the following 52 Key Words and then re-read this section on The Success Model. Each Key Word affects one of the five steps in The Success Model. Full comprehension of all 52 Key Words will enable you to apply The Success Model principles to your life.

Attitude

Any fact facing us is not as important as our attitude toward it, for that determines our success or failure.
- Dr. Norman Vincent Peale -Twentieth century author.

Our thoughts and images are responsible for how we feel. By filling our lives with positive thoughts and images, it is only natural that we will feel stronger and more dynamic. A positive attitude will enable us to get the most out of every opportunity.

Negative thinkers have difficulty seeing the positive outcome of any endeavor. This conflicts with everything The Success Model is built around. Negative thinkers are chronic procrastinators (see Procrastination). They are unable to implement a plan because they just won't start. Of course, there are going to be negative events that happen from time to time. You couldn't have positive without negative. Negative is reality. Don't ignore negative, but don't let it defeat you, either. Learn to deal with negativity.

There is a story of a city completely surrounded by a high wall. In the wall there was only one gate through which to enter and exit the city. An old man sat by the gate every day and children came from all over the city just to hear him tell stories. One day a man came by the city gate and said, "I have been traveling for several weeks and am looking for a new city to settle in. Are the people in this city very nice?" The old man paused and asked the traveler: "What were the people like in the city you left?" The traveler responded: "All the people where I used to live were mean and untrustworthy." The old man replied: "Then that is what you will find here." The traveler thanked the old man for his frankness and departed. The next day, another traveler came by the gate and spoke to the old man. He said, "I left the town where I used to live because my business failed and I am looking for a new city to live in. How are the people in your town?" The old man paused, and once again asked: "How were the people in your former town?" The traveler responded: "They were wonderful! They were all very friendly and sincere. If it had not been for business reasons, I would never have left." The old man replied: "Then that is what you will find here." The traveler thanked him and entered the city.

The children then asked the old man why he had lied and given the two travelers different descriptions of the people of the city. The man said he had not lied, because people will always get just what they look for. He explained that he had answered each traveler honestly, telling him that he would find the people of the city to be just as he expected them.

What makes a positive thinker? Positive thinking and acting starts with your physical being. The two biggest factors in a positive physical being are your smile and posture. By starting your day off with a smile, not only do you feel good but also you radiate that good feeling to your friends and associates. This enables you to keep those around you in a positive mode, thus making it easier for you to stay positive. Your erect posture is not only interpreted by others as a sign of confidence, it is also an inward signal that you are in charge and on a positive tract. If you slump, you feel weak and incapable. When you stand tall, you feel strong and in control.

Another key to maintaining a positive attitude is your ability to deal with negative people. Realize that negative thinkers just want others to "join the bandwagon," they perpetuate their negative attitude by getting other people to join in negative conversation. This is destructive and should be avoided. Instead, deal with the negative person and then move on as quickly as possible. After leaving a negative person, repeat a positive affirmation to yourself. For example, "My positive attitude will enable me to reach my goals and achieve the success I deserve."

When things go wrong and problems arise, you need to know that everyone has problems. So long as you are alive, you must deal with challenges. By facing challenges with a positive attitude, you are in a better position to create the solutions necessary to solve problems and move on. Successful people don't just face problems when they arise, they learn to anticipate them and prepare for them.

Listening to and reading positive material will help you to maintain and expand your positive mental outlook. After exposing yourself to outside positive material, you will find that your energy level will rise and your creative powers increase. An excellent way to get your day off to a good start is to listen to motivational and educational material in your car on the way to work. When you arrive, your energy level will be high and your creative self will already be addressing daily goals.

Some people dwell on all the things that have gone wrong in their lives. They think about accidents, layoffs, and other negative events. Other people, however, concentrate on the things they want to happen and what they can do to accomplish them. Since you can only process one thought at a time, if you are dealing with a negative attitude and dwelling on the past or on conditions you can't control, your efforts and energy will not be funneled in a direction that will yield positive results. However, if you can look beyond limitations and the negative aspects of life (which, by the way, are in everyone's life), then you can focus on your primary desires, have the right attitude, and work, with passion, to accomplish those desires.

Try to see the positive outcome of any meeting, sales situation, or challenge you may have. By seeing the eventual positive outcome, you will focus on that result and be in position to achieve it. Focus on the target, not on the obstacle. Often, a golfer will be so concerned with a sand trap that his shot will go directly into the sand trap, just as if he had aimed for it. He should have been concentrating on the green, his real goal and ultimate target. Don't you concentrate on the negative, on things you don't want, because many times you can't control them anyway. Instead concentrate on your primary desires. If you are working towards your primary desires, you will be working on those things you enjoy. Although you may not enjoy some of the associated tasks along the way, it's the ultimate results you are working for. You will find a way to achieve your primary desires if you apply the proper attitude.

The way you approach a situation, your attitude, will affect the way you act, and the way you act will affect the eventual outcome. With what type of attitude will you look at the situations in your life? I bought a pair of sunglasses to use for skiing. They came with an extra lens called a Persimmon lens. On an overcast day, with the persimmon lens installed, the snow instantly came alive. The increased brightness and clarity were amazing. Think about the effect this lens had on how I was able to view the snow. The lens did not generate more light, it only changed the way I perceived the light looked and how I was able to maneuver on the snow. Through what type of lens do you look at your surroundings? Does your lens, your attitude, brighten or darken your environment? Are you concentrating on the things you can control and focusing on your goals? Doing so will give you truly amazing results. Your positive attitude will enable you to overcome challenges faster and put you in a better position to move forward on your goals. Work hard every day to maintain a strong positive outlook on life.

Balance

Do you want my one-word secret of happiness? It's growth -
mental, financial, you name it.
- Harold S. Geneen -CEO IT&T.

By balancing the major areas of your life, you create
an inner harmony. Happiness is attained by achieving success in all of the major areas of our life. When one's financial success is overshadowed by the lack of success in other
important areas of life, imbalance results. If you create a terrific net worth but then find yourself sickly and unable to
enjoy your time and money, how happy will you be? How
successful will you really have been?

It is much easier to find your life out of balance than
in balance. It is only natural that when you list your primary desires, there is conflict. Balancing these desires is difficult. You will sometimes have to accept short-term imbalance to achieve long-term success and long-term balance.
Achievement of balance takes effort. In reaching successful
balance, however, you will enjoy a rewarding life in all areas
and one successful venture will be magnified by another.
You will attain emotional tranquility and be able to appreci-

ate and enjoy your continued successes. Balance does not mean equal time in all of life's important areas. Your business career will obviously require more time than your social life. Balance means recognizing that you have a variety of needs and working towards fulfilling those needs.

There are seven areas of life that need to be balanced:

Financial/Career	**Social**
Health	**Recreation**
Education	**Spiritual**
Family	

Financial/Career
>   Job (income source)
>   Security (investments, retirement)

Do enjoy your work? Are you in a position to earn the type of income that will enable you to do and see the things you want in life? The level of adequate income is different for each person. I can't tell you how much is enough. You have to decide that for yourself. Remember, money will not make you happy, but it will allow you to find out what will make you happy.

What is financial success? I believe that financial success is the ability to do the things in life that you want. It does not matter what those things are, as long as you can afford them. Obviously, this list of things will be different for each individual. One person may be happy taking a 14 foot bass boat to go fishing every Saturday. Another person may want a 65-foot cruiser to travel in the Caribbean. As long as they are able to afford the boat they want, they are both financially successful. You shouldn't set your financial goals based on other's expectations of you, but on your primary desires with respect to financial success. You can earn as much money as you would like. Your primary desire must be to earn that specific amount. However, don't chase dollars just to chase dollars. Don't neglect health, family, and the social, and spiritual areas of your life.

Many people don't realize how much easier financial success could be if they had a well thought out plan. Most Americans waste the opportunity to earn more than two times as much money in their lifetime as they get paid from their regular job. This may seem hard to believe but consider the following example. A person begins working at age 18 and then retires at age 65. If average annual salary during those 47 years is $30,000, then he/she will earn $1,510,000 in their lifetime. Now, say that same person saves 8% of their yearly earnings and invests it at a reasonable return. He/she would accumulate over $2,100,000 in savings by the age of 65. However, in reality the average person has well less than $100,000 at retirement. This person has spent or passed up the opportunity to earn over $3,500,000 in his/her lifetime, more than twice his/her annual earnings from direct work!

Your financial success will affect your level of success in other primary desires. Finances is one of the major reason for quarrels in a marriage. If having a successful family life and being a good father and understanding husband are important to you, then not arguing about finances is something for which you should strive. If travel is a primary desire (one that you are willing to "walk through fire for"), obviously you can travel further with ten-thousand-dollars than you can with one hundred. Your financial situation will effect all areas of your life.

Your financial potential is great. The exact amount of earnings and savings you receive will be dictated by your primary desires. You will only apply your energy, enthusiasm, passion and commitment to earn what your primary desires require. However, if you do that, you will be success.

Health
Diet
Exercise

Our bodies are remarkable machines that transport us through life's journey. Do you maintain your machine? I know a person who raises and shows pure-bred dogs. He earns a lot of money in breeding and puppy fees. His dogs are groomed daily, are on special diets, have regular exercise routines, and go to the veterinarian for regular checkups. He makes his living with his animals. If you raised valuable animals, would you feed them junk food or keep them up all hours of the night? Would you fill their water dish with alcohol or let them stay out in the rain and get sick? No you wouldn't. Nor should you do any of these things to yourself. Many people don't do well because they don't feel well, and they don't feel well because they haven't kept their bodies healthy.

Get on a good healthy diet. You don't have to be a

fanatic, just get educated. There are many good books on nutrition. Race cars run on super high octane fuel not low octane, engine knocking gasoline. A good low fat diet will help you lose weight and put your body in the low risk areas for many common health problems. Along with proper eating habits, a regular exercise routine is great not only for the cardio-vascular system, but it also releases endorphins into the blood stream. Endorphins cause a natural high and increase your energy level. You will find that a simple exercise program of 20 to 30 minutes, three to four times a week, will not only improve your health but also help relieve stress and maintain emotional balance. Of course, it is always a good idea to check with your doctor when making health decisions.

Education

You shouldn't feed your body junk food and you shouldn't let your brain atrophy. Limit the amount of television you watch. Read a good book, attend a seminar, or listen to training or motivational cassettes. Feed your brain the "good stuff" and your creativity will be jump-started and your energy level will rise. If you read just 35 pages a day, over the next ten years you will end up having read over 450 books! Imagine all the knowledge you will gain. How will this knowledge leave you with respect to your competition? It has been said that, "you will be judged by the books you read and the people you know." What books are **you** reading?

Family

Quality time with loved ones is very important. Your family deserves more than just bits and pieces of junk time. Children want to be noticed. They need recognition. So does your spouse. Your family is the important support base for your many journeys toward success. Reward your children and spouse for their efforts. Set aside specific amounts of time to participate in activities that **they** enjoy. If your children like the zoo, share that with them. If your spouse likes to see a good play or enjoys watching baseball, make a point of including those forms of entertainment in your schedule. Your family will appreciate your efforts to recognize and share their interests with them. Don't watch television and think you are spending time with them. Let your family know you value them and that their needs and goals are important to you also.

Social

The social arena of your life includes relationships with friends, organizational memberships and civic responsibilities. Having close, bonding relationships with friends can be rewarding from both an emotional standpoint as well as career development. Friends can provide a valuable source for consultation and sharing of life's events. In addition, in the business arena, friends can make excellent starting points for developing customers as well as providing referral business. Club memberships offer good business contacts. Civic involvement is also critical. You must give back to the system so it has more to give. By donating your time to worthwhile organizations or civic groups, others will benefit, and in the long run, so will you. Volunteering brings its own intrinsic reward. But the side benefits include making additional contacts that can lead to business and personal growth.

Recreation

The recreation area of life includes those areas of personal interest, whether they be, theater or traveling or sports. You may have primary desires relating to those and other recreational ideas. To really be happy it is necessary to pursue your personal recreation interests. By satisfying the recreational area of life, you are allowing yourself to enjoy some of the fun things you may have always dreamt about. Now is the time to list those interests and pursue them!

Spiritual

The spiritual aspects of life are related to humanities timeless connection to organized systems of ethics and your personal value system. It is not for me to preach religion but I believe that spiritual involvement can be a very moving and important part of anyone's life. A belief in a traditional spiritual value system can serve both as a guide and as an inspiration. The rewards you get are determined by the efforts you make. It's all up to you. The important thing is, if you believe in something spiritual don't neglect it.

By balancing these seven major areas, you will achieve a high level of success and personal happiness.

Success in one area without the others will leave you unfulfilled and seeking something else to make you happy. People who balance these aspects of their lives can fully enjoy their successes and maximize the satisfaction they receive from the positive events in their lives. What good would a large bank account be if you couldn't take the time to enjoy some recreation? What good would success in any area be if you didn't have family or friends to share it with? The seven areas of life are intertwined. The results you achieve in one area are heightened by the results achieved in another.

When I go skiing, it is a great opportunity to get away from more stressful activities. I always return from a skiing trip renewed and full of energy. My performance in business, my attitude around the house, and my enthusiasm for running are all peaked by my having enjoyed one of my recreational interests. Life should be about fulfillment, fulfillment of primary desires.

Believe

Your belief that you can do the thing gives your thought forces their power.
- Robert Collier -Nineteenth century American author.

You must believe in yourself and your abilities. You must believe in your thinking. Most of all, you must believe in your mission. You must believe that what you are doing is right and good. Over time, your actions will lead to the desired benefits and results. You must continue to have confidence and believe in yourself when others doubt you. Your conviction is not only what moves you, but it is also what moves other people. Your inner belief will be infectious. This will help you recruit others to assist you in the achievement of your goals.

Selling, for example, is the effective transfer of enthusiasm from the salesperson to the prospect. Your total belief in what you are and what you do will enhance your enthusiasm and promote its positive transfer. This will result in more sales.

Building inner belief is, in essence, building stronger

self-esteem. If you don't believe in yourself, you won't try, and failure is guaranteed before you even start. People with high self-esteem achieve their highest goals. Lack of proper self-esteem is why others settle for mediocrity. You will not attempt a goal unless you believe you can accomplish it. Your fear of failure and rejection will inhibit you from taking action. If, on the other hand, you know and believe that anything is possible, you will attempt the task and probably succeed.

For example, children will not open drawers if they don't believe they can open them. However, once you show children they can open a drawer, they will open every drawer in sight. The child already had the ability to open the drawer, he/she just did not know it. Children who believe in their ability get results. It is the same with adults.

You will never know what you can accomplish, you'll never achieve any goal, unless you try. Only by *starting* on the journey can you hope to arrive at the final destination. Your ability to start the journey is directly related to your belief in your current skills or your ability to gain the skills necessary to complete the task. If you believe you can, you will.

Commitment

The person who makes a success of living is the one who sees his goal steadily and aims for it unswervingly. That is dedication.
- Cecil B. De Mille -Filmmaker.

Your level of commitment is going to be related to your level of desire. You must have personal commitment to be able to move forward toward your goals. Only primary desires will generate the high level of commitment necessary to see you through. You need a high degree of "stick-with-it-ness." It is this commitment to your achievement that will enable you to take the steps necessary to reach your goals and become a master achiever.

> *Don't think of success in terms of time but rather in terms of results.*

Many people say, "I'll give this program three months to see if it works." Well, what if it takes four months, or six months, or a year? You can't be sure how long it will take to achieve the results of your primary desires. It's not that you are looking to spend three months, it's that you are looking for specific results, the achievement of your primary desires. That's what matters. And whatever it takes to get to that point is what you must be willing to do. If you're not, it's not a genuine primary desire. It is not something you are willing to "walk through fire for". If your goals are based only on your *primary* desires, then you will have the necessary energy and commitment to complete your goals and reach the success you want. By thinking of success in terms of results, you will concentrate all your energy and effort on those results and you will do whatever it takes to get them and the success that goes along with them.

You must convert your desire for success into a commitment to win by paying a daily price for long term success. When I was in school, it seemed as if it was going to be forever before I graduated. Then once I graduated and I looked back on my time in school, it seemed as if it only lasted a short time. A year has 365 days no matter whether you are looking forward or backward. However, often when we look back in time the days seem short and flow together. I call this *The Past Value of Time*. Time that has passed is usually looked upon as brief. As you work toward your goals, future success might seem years and years away. But when you reach success, it will seem as if it happened overnight. Remember this concept when the future seems very distant. The Past Value of Time will make the days and weeks and months, even years of effort, seem short in duration. Let this knowledge comfort you as you push ahead.

Sometimes people mistakenly give up on their mission just before the rewards are reaped. Remember the cliché; "It's always darkest before the dawn." By having the fortitude to stay with your plan, you will be able to excel when others have not.

Many people want to be sure of something before they commit themselves to it. However, I don't believe you can be sure. I believe that you won't know if it can work *until* you commit yourself to it.

I have said or implied several times that the ability to achieve is inherent in us all. The successful people of this world have learned and taken the steps necessary to get what it is they want. They know that if they stick with this proven system, the positive outcome is inevitable. Be committed!

Creativity

Ideas are the root of creation.
- Ernest Dimnet -Twentieth century writer and lecturer.

Creativity is the ability to generate answers to questions or solutions to problems, that when implemented, will move you closer to achieving your primary desires. Real achievers are those people that exhibit the highest degree of creativity. Creativity is an ability that all of us share. The difference between individuals who display creativity and those who don't is the ability to encourage creative impulses and then take action on their creative thoughts. Creativity will help set you apart from the crowd and add momentum to a stalled situation. While some people get caught up in the dilemma of, "Whether the cup is half empty or half full," I want to figure out a way to make the cup bigger!

Once I was working with a potentially large window customer who had a tough time making decisions. My presentations, phone conversations, thank you notes, and follow-up correspondence had established good rapport between this client and myself. It was time for him to commit to my program for the new year. His business represented over $1 million in sales and I wanted it, but I just couldn't seem to pull him off the fence. He knew it was time to make the decision and seemed to be avoiding my calls. It was now or never. Rather than letting this customer get away I used creativity to increase my effectiveness and get the business. I had an audio tape written and produced by an advertising company. I filled it with great sound effects. The tape described a sweepstakes and all the prizes available if the listener would just call. However as each prize was identified the sound of breaking glass covered up the exact detail of the prize. The last message on the tape instructed the listener to call me at my private phone number. I put the tape in a portable tape player, complete with headset and cover letter, and mailed it to my customer, next day delivery. The next day my phone rang and all I heard was laughter. The client was mine! I got the order for a million dollar account! Instead of being stifled, I let my building anxiety trigger my creativity, enabling me to move forward on my goal. It is in challenging situations such as this that the need for creativity is greatest.

Creativity comes from positive energy. Your desire to move ahead should be stronger then your frustration at being bogged down. Becoming more creative is the outcome of paying attention to the endless stream of ideas you have, recording them, and then applying them when the time is right.

Not long ago a young Hollywood actress, after she had trouble finding an agent to represent her, became her own agent. She needed an aggressive agent to get her acting jobs. When a traditional agent could not be found, she decided to take matters into her own hands. She used an assumed name and acquired a fake accent. She used her answering machine to create the atmosphere of a large and very successful agency. The message told which agents could be reached in the New York office or the London office on any particular day. Of course, those offices did not even exist. However, the results were great. She got screenings and acting jobs over a four year period. Her creativity had enabled her to get through to all the big directors and casting personnel.

The following illustration shows how the creative process works. ***Question plus sponge plus egg equals ideas.***

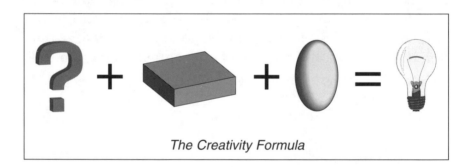

The Creativity Formula

The creative process begins with a question. You seek an answer to a question or a solution to a problem. Then, just as a sponge soaks up water, you should "soak up" information. Constantly expose yourself to new concepts and input on your desired topic. For an egg to hatch it must incubate, so must your thoughts. This process can take minutes, hours, or even weeks. With the right amount of incubation time, your light bulbs will turn on. You may find yourself sitting up in the middle of the night with the solution to a problem or the answer may come as you drive down the street. The more information you have to process the more material your subconscious mind can draw on to create news ideas. Give it time. The creative thoughts will come.

People who are not creative do not lack creative skills, they just don't ask "why?" They do not question what appears to be the status quo. They accept things the way they are and take things for face value. They say: "This is the way it is, so this is the way it must be." Instead, they should ask: "Why is it this way? Can we do it better? Is there another approach to this situation?"

It is amazing how creative children can be. Children have not yet formed set ideas about the way things "have" to be. They are always questioning. The average four year old asks 437 questions a day! It's this questioning that leads to their creativity and gives them the ability to come up with solutions to problems that, sometimes, adults can't see.

Creativity is *fleeting*. Many people have creative ideas but don't write them down and can't remember them later. When an idea "pops" into your head, make a note of it right away. You can decide whether or not to act on it at a later time. For example, in February, I always seem to think of something that would be perfect for my wife's birthday. However, when her birthday comes around in September, my mind won't produce any good ideas. Now, I've learned to write down any gift ideas when I think of them. I have a page in my planner just for that purpose.

Daydreaming is a good way of freeing your subconscious to process your ideas. Sometimes some of my best ideas occur when I attend obligatory luncheons or when listening to speakers who are not very interesting. Always keep something with you so that you can record your ideas.

Creative solutions can come from unusual sources. Read books on subjects that are new to you. Attend lectures on topics outside your normal business interest. You will be amazed at the new ideas that are generated this way and which can be *combined* with your current knowledge in new and creative ways.

Your degree to which you are considered unique is a result of your applied creativity. Being unique means you are more likely to get an opportunity in a competitive situation. Prior to finishing graduate school, I scheduled job interviews with seven of the top public accounting firms. The graduating class was given instructions on interviewing and we were told to keep our resumes to one page, since the interviewer would not want to flip back and forth between stapled pages. Technically, I followed the rules, but with a little creative twist. I used an 11 X 17 sheet of paper, folded in half to the standard 8.5 X 11. The interviewer didn't have to flip pages but when opened like a book, my resume had twice the space for including all the important information about myself. I also placed my photograph on the cover of my resume (unheard of at the time). I figured that, although my resume and interview would provide all the necessary information, after three days of 30-minute interviews an interviewer might have trouble remembering one candidate from another. I didn't want to be forgotten and I wasn't! I was called back for second interviews by all of the companies and received offers for employment very early in the process. It would be nice to think that it was my outstanding grades that did the trick, but I know better. It was my willingness to go with my creative impulses to put together a functional yet *unique* resume that helped me achieve my desired results.

Encourage your creativity. Ask questions. Acquire new and different information. The ideas will come. When they do, go with them. Trust and believe in them (see Believe). Superior creativity yields superior results.

Crisis

Crises refine life. In them you discover what you are.
- Allan K. Chalmers -Twentieth century American author.

Crisis is inevitable. The question is not *if* it will happen; the question is *when*. When a crisis does arrive how will you handle it? Will you have anticipated the problem and make some kind of preparation?

Remember, each time you emerge from a crisis you are stronger and better equipped to succeed than you were before. For example to harden steel, it is heated to temperatures as high as 1700° F. Then it is placed in a cold bath. This is a form of stress or crisis. This tempering process hardens the steel and makes it twice as strong. When you face a crisis, it's as if *you* are being tempered. When you conquer a crisis, you emerge stronger than you were before.

Crises can be approached two ways:

Reactively
Proactively

The actions of reactive people are shaped by what has already happened in their environment. On the other hand, the actions of proactive people are based on their values and beliefs. Proactive people determine the broad scope of circumstances for any given event in their lives. Reactive people play the game of life, using rules that were set down by others. Proactive people, however, play by their own set of rules, based on their own value system. While reactive people respond to the ringing phone, emergencies, and requests for help from others, proactive people decide what they want to accomplish in a given day. Their list of tasks is based on *their* primary desires and their values determine what is important and how life's issues are prioritized.

If you are proactive and driven by a set of well-thought out beliefs, you will be able to raise significantly your level of accomplishment. You will accomplish what *you* want to accomplish. You will be more effective and more productive, thereby getting the results *you* want.

The proactive approach means anticipating the challenges and problems you may encounter during the execution of your plan. This will enable you to eliminate a crisis in some cases and, in others, be prepared with a well thought-out plan of action. By planning in advance, you can make better decisions because you will be doing your thinking *without* the pressure of a crisis situation. In addition, you will not lose valuable time thinking about what to do. You will be prepared to act.

Sometimes, unfortunately, you are forced to react. A crisis is upon you and you must deal with it. When this happens, you need to be equipped.

I spell equip "**ECIP**," which stands for:

Evaluate
Create
Implement
Proceed

Evaluate the situation. Assess what is really happening and how it affects you and your goals. Is this situation really a crisis? The last thing you want to do is overreact to a situation that maybe you could just as well bypass. If you treat a normal situation as a crisis, you will be wasting valuable creative energy on an event that doesn't warrant it. In addition, your focus will be on the "false alarm" and not on the objectives of your plan. The evaluation stage will also give you the opportunity to gather information necessary to formulate a plan should it really turn out to be a crisis.

Of my four children, the youngest is the one that is always getting into things. Allison's gross motor skills developed unbelievably fast. She could leap tall buildings in a single bound. At the age of two she was into everything. From time to time, you could hear her 7-year old sister Sara yelling from the back of the house: " *Emergency! Emergency!*" When I heard those cries, I stopped whatever I was doing, wherever I was, and rushed to find Allison. Sometimes, Allison was in a dangerous situation hanging onto a shelf. At those times, I was glad that I had almost broken my neck to arrive in time. At other times, Allison had just made a huge mess and it was not a true emergency. Evaluate the situation before you declare it a crisis.

Using *creativity*, built on positive energy, you will be able to devise solutions to the challenges at hand. By concentrating on creative solutions, your energy level will rise. This will enable you to work through the crisis situation. Solutions can come from within. Many people underestimate their own ability to deal with emergencies. Discussing problems with others can provide solutions, too (see Mentor). Is there someone who has faced this situation before? Can you learn from someone else's experiences? Remember, there's no need to reinvent the wheel. Most successful people are willing to share experiences. They remember what they went through to reach their goals and they are willing to help others who show similar initiative. Take advantage of this valuable resource. By discussing crises with outsiders, you'll be able to get opinions that are unbiased. A mentor will be able to view the situation without being blinded by emotion. Be careful to seek advice from someone who has the education or experiences to give qualified advice. For example, although, I have over twenty years experience in sales and management, I would not give a physicist advice concerning nuclear science. However, I could certainly offer valuable information and assistance to someone who was seeking help in management, sales or success techniques.

Implementing your creative solutions will help you on your journey to success. This is where you *make it happen*. Implementation requires a high level of energy for a short period of time. Your degree of commitment will determine your ability to face these challenges and endure.

Proceed with your original plan and recognize that you can be stronger for having experienced the crisis. Don't deal with problems any longer than necessary. Once your plan has been implemented and the crisis resolved, turn your focus to your main objectives. ***Get back on track.***

Some times in the course of a presentation a salesperson will meet with an objection. Unfortunately, after dealing with the objection, they will fail to move on. This hesitation allows the customer to bring up another objection, and then another. Eventually, the sale will be lost. Remember after dealing with the crisis or objection, move on with your agenda.

When training to qualify for my first Boston Marathon, I ran 24-mile workouts. Once at about the 18 mile point, I started feeling tired and as though I were starting to dehydrate. Every muscle in my body ached. I wanted to end the workout but I was four miles from home and didn't even have a quarter to make a phone call. So, I formed a plan. I changed both my pace and my form and I started to run more freely. I finished the workout and felt great. Not only did I finish the workout but also on race day, I ran the time I needed to fulfill my goal and qualify for the Boston Marathon.

The crisis during my workout had made me stronger. I had gained new-found confidence that positively effected my ability to successfully achieve my goal.

What if you owned a retail store and heard that a similar store was opening up in the same shopping center? The first thing to do would be to confirm the facts. If the story isn't true, don't waste your time worrying about something that isn't going to happen. If a competitor is moving in, develop a plan of action. You might increase advertising or start a buyer's club to hold onto existing customers before the new store opened. Once your plan is devised, implement it at once. Waiting will only cost you money in this situation. Once the crisis handling plan to handle the crisis is executed, continue implementing your original plan, aimed at your primary desires. Don't spend time worrying about "what if's." If you have dealt with the situation to the best of your ability, focus on the plans that will lead you to the actualization of your primary desires.

By effectively handling any crisis that occurs during the implementation phase of The Success Model, you will maintain your momentum and move closer to the achievement of your primary desires.

Discipline

You never will be the person you can be if pressure, tension, and discipline are taken out of your life.
- James G. Bilkey -Nineteenth century British author.

> *Anyone can have a dream; it takes*
> *discipline to make it reality.*

If you don't have the self discipline to learn and live the philosophy presented here, you will have trouble being a real achiever. It takes effort to enact each key word in this book. Some of the steps in The Success Model take a dedication that is greater than you have ever had to exhibit before. Discipline will enable you to do the things that you need to do and it will keep you from being distracted by things that take you away from the achievement you are striving for.

Self-discipline is a balancing act of emotions and logic. Sometimes you may be torn between things that you want to do and things that you need to do in order to progress on your plan. People around you may use emotions to try to influence you. But if you have the appropriate balance you will be able to minimize the emotional impact and instead use logic to determine your actions.

Ultimately, discipline will come as a result of your working on your primary desires. It is the strength and intensity of those desires that will generate self-discipline. You must want the results of your plan more than anything else in order to have the discipline to follow through.

Recognizing the need for and importance of self-discipline is critical. With this knowledge in hand, you will know what actions to look for in your daily routine. Do you have the self-discipline necessary to achieve your goals? Are you willing to forgo other pleasures to insure the attainment of your primary desires? Self-discipline will help you achieve greatness. The lack of self-discipline will lead you to mediocrity. Do what it takes to implement your plan and you can attain the greatness you deserve.

Enthusiasm

Every great and commanding movement in the annals of the world is the triumph of enthusiasm. Nothing great was ever achieved without it.
- Ralph Waldo Emerson -Nineteenth century American writer.

When someone has a feast, they really do it up. The table is set with all the trimmings. There might be two or three main courses, several different salads, various fruits and vegetables, and of course an incessant assortment of desserts. The service too, would be impeccable. Someone would pick up plates as soon as you finished eating a course. Your glass would be immediately filled after you drank from it. A feast is a wonderful way to dine.

On the other hand, some people are forced to fast for a variety of reasons. They must abstain from certain or all types of food. In a fast, there are no choices of main courses, no fancy table, and no desserts. And, of course, there is no service. Notice that the only difference between the word **FEAST**, which is highly desirable, and the word **FAST**, which is undesirable, is the letter "E." Here, I believe the "E" stands for **enthusiasm**.

The word enthusiasm comes from the Greek word "Enthousiasmos," which means "breath of life." There must be life in everything you do to get the results you want. When you breath life into a job or a task, you are going to enjoy doing it because you know it will help you achieve a primary desire. That's a great feeling. How many people do you know work at a job day after day and week after week that they dislike or just don't enjoy? The best way to generate a high level of enthusiasm and enjoyment for a job or task is to know you are working toward a primary desire.

The right amount of enthusiasm can move mountains. As I have stated before, a good salesperson can effectively transfer his enthusiasm to the customer. When the customer becomes enthusiastic about a product or service, the sale is practically closed. It is the energy, derived from enthusiasm, that drives the sale. That same energy will drive you to do what is necessary to achieve your primary desires. Not only will your enthusiasm drive you forward, it will also enable you to do a great job at what it is that needs to be done in order to be a success.

Put enthusiasm into everything you do. It will become contagious to those around you. Your actions will be supercharged and the results ever greater than anticipated.

Expectations

Few enterprises of great labor or hazard would be undertaken if we had not the power of magnifying the advantages we expect from them.

- Samuel Johnson -Eighteenth century British writer and lexicographer.

If you raise your expectations to a certain level then you will require yourself to perform at that level. When you demand more of yourself you will be surprised by how strong you will perform to satisfy those demands. If you place forty-thousand-dollar expectations upon yourself, you will seek forty-thousand-dollar results. If you have one-hundred-thousand-dollar expectations, you will work toward one-hundred-thousand-dollar results. You must however believe that your expectations should be at this new, higher level. For when you buy into the higher value, and raise your expectations, you will be able to perform at this level.

I learned how to ski with four friends at a small skiing area just outside of St. Louis. In an introductory 30-minute lesson, we learned how to put our skis on, stand up, and make a rough turn. We were advised to stay on the easy (practically flat) slope the rest of the day and practice our turns. In a short time, of course we felt somewhat "experienced" and began to eye the main runs and chair lift. So, we decided to go for it. Once at the top of the chair lift, however, we worked our way over to the edge of the run and looked down. Although it was sleeting and the wind was blowing, the four of us were immersed in total silence. It seemed as if we were trying to ski Mount Everest! A ski lift, of course, is a one-way operation; you can ride up, but you can't ride down. It is at this point, you can imagine, that I raised my expectations with regards to my skiing ability. I could only go in one direction. And guess what? I came through. I raised my level of performance to meet the challenge. *Now* I won't say that it was pretty or even skillful, but I did ski down the hill and I made it to the bottom in one piece. From then on, the next "impossible" thing was easier. And the time after that, it was easier. Again and again.

How can you raise your level of expectations in the seven basic areas of your life? Think about them: financial/career, health, education, family, social, recreation, and spiritual. What would your life be like if your were able to increase your performance just ten percent in each of these areas? Now, apply the success model to these new expectations. Think about the changes you will make to accomplish these new, higher levels of performance. Outline plans using your creative process and then begin implementing those plans today. You can and will achieve more than you ever thought possible.

Raise your level of expectation. Put yourself in a situation that forces you to move towards your goals. You'll be pleased with the results.

Failure

He's no failure. He's not dead yet.
- William Lloyd George -Author.

I believe that it is theoretically possible for a person to go through life without ever failing. This might sound impossible on the surface, but let's look deeper.

To understand failure, we need to review certain definitions. Success is the results received from your daily achievements in pursuit of your primary desires. I define failure as *quitting*. It's that simple. In-between the attainment of your desired results and failure there is the gray area that I call "less than desired results." Most people fail because they give up, or quit, when they get less than desired results. The following story may help clarify the relationship of success, failure and less than desired results.

Jane worked in the printing business and desired to be in business for herself. It seemed natural to open a small print shop. She scraped together some money, made a small business loan, and purchased the equipment necessary to open her shop. After one year, sales were not what Jane had projected and her funds were running out. Jane's notes were coming due and she was unable to pay them. Her daughter, who was in high school, asked her to print some flyers for the homecoming football game. Jane came up with an idea. She purchased 250 cotton T-shirts and on them printed:

Homecoming Weekend
October 18-20
"Catch the Spirit"

The shirts were a huge success and she sold every one. With the proceeds from those shirts, she bought more shirts and began soliciting other high schools. Shirt sales were so brisk that Jane sold her traditional printing presses and bought better silk-screening equipment. Sales contin-ued to soar. She begin printing team uniforms. Before long, her business grew to be one of the largest sports specialty stores in the state!

What a success story. Compare that to what might have happened if Jane had quit the business before she got the T-shirt idea. She would have been a failure. Instead of quitting, Jane **modified** her plans and pushed forward. Although, at first she had less than desirable results, she knew he could achieve her primary desire of owning her own successful business if she didn't give up.

Don't you give up. You may not always have the results you desire at first, but if you move forward, you can and will obtain positive results. Failure will only come to those who mistakenly or knowingly decide to quit. Your success may be different than originally expected, but it will come, and you will enjoy it.

Faith

Faith is to believe what we do not see; and the reward of this faith is to see what we believe.
- St. Augustine -Fourth century Bishop.

In order to achieve, you will need assistance from others, additional capital, new skills and other things that you do not already have. Start your quest now. Have faith that the things you need will present themselves along the way. When you write down and commit yourself to achieving a personal desire, you will be amazed by the people who will come into your life.

In the early eighties when I traveled extensively selling wholesale women's fashion accessories, I would enter a new town and need directions to the store I was seeking. It always seemed as if the main street I needed to turn on never came up. I would backtrack, thinking I had missed it, and then end up backtracking again to find the street. Finally, I developed the philosophy of following all directions with supreme faith. I knew the street I needed to turn on would arrive if I kept going. It usually did.

It is 1,956 miles from St. Louis to Los Angeles. My car will only go 360 miles on a tank of gas, which means that I will still need to travel another 1,500 miles when I run out of gas. This knowledge does not keep me from starting my trip. And guess what? I am able to get all the way to the west coast and not run out of gas. You see, I know that along the way I will be presented with gasoline stations where I can get more gas. I don't know where these gasoline stations will be but I know they are out there. I have faith.

When I started this book, I only had one friend who had written a book. I had no writing experience and no contacts in the publishing industry. Along the way, people started showing up. Ken Blanchard consented to review my book. Magazine editors offered their assistance. Prominent speakers and others in the motivation and education field seemingly came out of nowhere to share their knowledge and provide valuable ideas, and help. I had the faith that I would find the answers to my questions, meet the people I needed, and publish my book. That is just what happened.

Faith can be a strong ally. Forge ahead. The most amazing things will happen in your life as you work toward your primary desires. Have faith!

Fear

He who fears being conquered is sure of defeat.
- Napoleon Bonaparte -Eighteenth century French emperor.

Many people never pursue their primary desires because they live with worry and fear. Worry clutters the mind. Your brain can only process one thought at a time. If it is busy worrying, it can't be busy generating creative solutions to problems. Free your mind to do the most productive things possible. Consciously or unconsciously, you will get and become what you think about. If you are thinking about problems and catastrophes, that is what will happen. If on the other hand, you concentrate on results, you will achieve results. Focus on your primary desires. Let your enthusiasm and energy spark your creativity so that you can develop solutions to problems.

Fear is a killer of greatness. The human mind can easily take a small fear and build it up to insurmountable proportions. Most of the time, after we have faced a fear and moved on, we find that the situation "wasn't as bad as we thought it would be." A child often dreads going to the doctor to get a shot and usually, however, when they leave they think: "That wasn't so bad." The same thing can be said about most of our fears. Fears, for the most part, are not life threatening, but we allow them to take the life out of us. Most of our worries are about things that never happen.

When I was in college one of my friends wanted to ask out this particular girl, but he was afraid she'd turn him down. So, he never asked her out. Rather than face her ***possible*** rejection, he accepted his ***definite*** rejection. He passed up the chance for a relationship that might have changed his life because he gave into fear.

You can't win unless you are willing to lose. I'm not saying that you should want to lose, but you will have to take some risks in order to have the opportunity to succeed If you do your homework, prepare yourself properly, and put yourself in a position to win, most times you will win!

In marathon racing there is a term called "hitting the wall." Hitting the wall is what happens when a runner totally runs out of glycogen (energy stored in your muscles). This happens when a runner maintains too fast a pace throughout the race. When a runner tries to lower his time, he must take a chance. By pushing the pace faster than he has run before he risks "hitting the wall." If he hits the wall, he may not be able to finish the race at all, much less finish it in record time. But if he never ever pushes himself, his time will never improve. By proper preparation and training, by taking a chance, he can achieve the breakthrough he is seeking and set a personal record.

Babies have to learn almost everything, although they are born with certain reflexes and fears. For example, a baby has a "grip" reflex that is very strong. The only fears a baby is born with are the fear of falling and the fear of loud sounds. All other fears are learned. If we can learn a fear, we can also learn to overcome that fear.

There are five major fears that deserve attention.

Fear of failure is the fear that you will not succeed in your mission or reach your goals. Through self talk we must develop the thought process that to have never tried is a worse failure than not properly executing your plan for success. You haven't failed until you quit. Up until that point you may have setbacks and have to make adjustments in your plan but you are still working towards your ultimate success.

Fear of rejection has kept many people from achieving their ultimate potential. They fear the word **no**. What they don't understand is that it may take many "no's" to get to one "yes," and one "yes" could be worth a fortune. It is the "yeses" we are after and the "no's" are just steps along the way.

Fear of the unknown is the fear of what *might* happen. Many times people get too caught up with worrying about long-shot possibilities instead of moving ahead and concentrating on doing a good job at achieving their primary desires.

Fear of success is the concern of moving away from our peer group, of getting out of our comfort zone. Success brings new relationships and new surroundings. Many people fear the outcome of success instead of concentrating on managing success.

Fear of change again moves us to an unfamiliar area. Sometimes it may seem easier to maintain your present status instead of dealing with the change necessary to implement The Success Model. This kind of thinking is short-sighted. The rewards of success will be greater than any short-term discomfort caused by temporary changes.

The *FUD* factor, **f**ear, **u**ncertainty and **d**oubt has kept many people from reaching their full potential.

> **F**ear
> **U**ncertainty
> **D**oubt

I know a woman who needs to finish just three papers in order to complete her college degree. One paper needs to be only five pages long. The woman admits that 75% of the research work necessary to complete the papers has already been done. She has been told at many interviews that certain jobs are not available to her without her college degree. But, it has been ten years since this woman left college! Her fear of success and of the unknown has kept her from getting a good job and enabling her to find out what she really wants in life. She has many unfulfilled primary desires because she has let her fears control her life.

Fears are powerful negative motivators. If we are to achieve greatness, we must overcome our fears. **Before we can overcome our fears, we must acknowledge their presence.** That doesn't mean that we have to accept them, just that we recognize that fear exists, that fears are normal, and that we have the ability to overcome fear .

One method of overcoming fear is programming our subconscious through auto-suggestion. Ask yourself: "What's the worst that can happen?" Most likely, you will never experience the worst in any situation. Nevertheless, in your mind's eye see yourself overcoming your fears. See yourself doing whatever it is you have feared. By imagining several successful experiences of overcoming your fears, your mind will gradually make the transition between an imagined positive experience and a real one.

Another way to overcome fear is to actually do what it is that you fear. By doing what you fear, your fears disappear. The greatest security in life can be yours by overcoming your fears and achieving the goals you set out to accomplish. Mark Twain once said, "Make it a point to do something every day that you don't want to do. This is the golden rule for acquiring the habit of doing your duty without pain." The greater risk is to do nothing.

A recent poll revealed that the fear of death was the second most common fear. The number one fear was having to speak in front of a large crowd. Some people say they would rather die than have to speak in front of a group. **The Dale Carnegie Center of Excellence uses a technique called *tagging* to help people overcome this fear.** Tagging can be applied to other fears as well.

Think of a time when you were either extremely happy or very successful. Maybe it was when you closed a sale that you had worked hard for, or maybe it was your graduation, wedding, or the first time you completed a 10K race. Recall the feelings you had: happiness, excitement, anticipation. Did your heart race? Were you smiling from ear to ear? Did you feel as if you could take on the whole world? Now, take those feelings and attach them to the task you want to do. In other words, know that your pending activity will produce those same feelings. You want to feel that way again, don't you? Tell yourself you can and will have those great feelings when you take on this task at hand. Tag this new task with the feelings and emotions of the previous great experience. Your inner mind wants those feelings to reoccur and they will!

To help you overcome your fears by doing what it is you fear most, *tag* the activity with the same emotions you experienced with an earlier successful, enjoyable experience.

Your primary desires, those desires you are willing to "walk through fire for," will give you the energy and courage to face your fears and overcome them. Let the power of your desires fill your mind and use this force to address and conquer any fears you may have. Imagine what you could achieve if you had no fear. Approach life as if your fears didn't exist, and then deal with them because nothing could be as bad as an unfulfilled dream.

Feedback

He who stops being better stops being good.
- Oliver Cromwell -Seventeenth century English military leader.

People like to know where they stand. Employees need to know if they are doing a good job. If a customer registers a complaint with you or someone in your company, it's not enough to deal with the problem. Customers want to know what steps are being taken on their behalf. Sometimes, actions are not enough. Tell them what you are doing. Feedback is a way to say "Keep up the good work" or "We need to see some improvement if we are to continue in this direction." Customers want to know that you've changed the way quality is checked or that you have instituted a new one week delivery program on their behalf.

It is also important to provide yourself feedback on your performances and progress toward your goals. After each sales call, a salesperson should evaluate the positive and negative aspects of the meeting and use that feedback to improve. A student should review a returned exam or paper and think about how he/she could have made improvements. You should evaluate your progress on your plans and be able to make adjustments.

You need feedback in order to keep you on track and moving toward your goals. Personal feedback can be obtained simply by asking questions. If you lose a customer, find out why. If you get a new customer, find out why. Only through proper questioning can you get the information necessary to repeat good performances and discontinue bad performances.

Good feedback will provide the information you need to maximize your good efforts and help you repeat desired performances. Good feedback will help you reduce negative outcomes in the future. Concentrate on providing a continual flow of feedback.

Focus

Consider the postage stamp: its usefulness consists in the ability to stick to one thing till it gets there.
- Josh Billings -Published in Farmers Almanac 1869-1880.

A study at Stanford University of genius-level children revealed some interesting information. The children were studied throughout their lifetime. The study showed that high achievement was not a consequence of high intelligence but rather the result of people who were able to focus sharply on what they wanted in life. The people that were better focused achieved more.

To stay focused, you must concentrate on the task at hand. Think about work when you are working, about play when you are playing, and about your family when you are with your family. You will perform at a sub-par level in every endeavor if you are not 100% involved at the moment of "attack."

Like the archer, you should be keying in on the bulls-eye. You must focus on your target. You do not want to spray arrows (or efforts and energy) in a multitude of different directions. You want your efforts going towards the bullseye, your goals. You must have the proper focus in order to follow the steps in your plan. This will help you reach your ultimate goal. If you are busy running haphazardly from one goal to another you lack the focus to accomplish anything. Some people fall into the trap of doing many things with mediocre results without doing anything exceptionally well.

Thomas Edison had 1093 inventions patented. When asked what was the key to his success and unusually high productivity, he said that he worked on only one project at a time and stayed on that project all day. He didn't move from project to project. He stayed focused.

When you find that you are having trouble staying focused, make a list of all your distractions. Evaluate each item one at a time and decide if it is something that really needs your attention. Then, if it must be acted on, decide if you must act or someone else can deal with it. You will find that many distractions can be eliminated, allowing you to focus on your primary desires.

Have you ever played Pin The Tail On The Donkey? In this game a blindfolded child attempts to place a tail on a picture of a donkey hanging on the wall. When the children have the blindfolds on, the tails can end up all over the room on windows, doors, lamps etc. If the child can see, however, the tail goes right where it belongs, on the end of the donkey. It stands to reason, if you can focus on your target, you can hit it. Likewise if you can't see what you desire, or if your attention and focus is on something else, you will not be able to achieve what you originally set out after.

When a major league baseball player is in a batting slump, people say: "He isn't seeing the ball real well." Sure, a batter's stance and technique are important, but if he doesn't keep his eye on the ball, he'll never hit it. Hitting a small ball coming toward him at over 90 mph requires the batter to have exceptional focus.

Your desires are just like that baseball moving at 90 mph. Don't be distracted by someone selling cotton candy on the sidelines. Watch the ball. Focus on your goals and stay with your plan. You can and will achieve everything you desire.

Fundamentals

If you would be remembered, do one thing superbly well.
- Saunders Norvell -Industrialist.

In any endeavor there are basic ideas that need to be comprehended. In order to succeed, you must understand and master these fundamentals.

If you wanted to play baseball, you would need to know how to throw, hit, catch, and run. You also need to know the rules. Those are the fundamentals. Sure, there are other skills that would be helpful, but being able to do these five things well would almost guarantee your success. Baseball managers know the value of fundamentals so well that they focus almost two whole months of spring training on them.

The Success Model is made up of five key components. By dividing success into Desire, Change, Plans, Implementation and Success, you have five smaller areas to master in order to achieve the results you desire.

Let's say you want to open a bookstore. What are the four or five things you should concentrate on?

Purchasing/Inventory Control
Marketing/Promotion
Display
Record Keeping
Personnel

You may find that each of these four areas could be broken down into its own set of four or five things to work on.

Purchasing/Inventory Control
    -Determine best suppliers.
    -Research yearly industry sales trends.
    -Establish re-order quantities.
    -Install computer system to assist with inventory.

Marketing/Promotion
    -Establish marketing budget.
    -Research what types of advertising your
     competition does.
    -Create a marketing plan.
    -Establish rapport with an advertising agency.

Display
    -Research what other bookstores use for displays.
    -Based on the size of your store and the look you
     want to achieve, determine the type of shelving
     you will need.
    -Learn about and obtain signage.

Record Keeping
    -Establish a bookkeeping system.
    -Research computer software available for
     bookstores.
    -Have your accountant review your choice of
     software and hardware.
    -Have the system installed.

Personnel
    -Study effective personnel management.
    -Determine personnel requirements based on
     hours of operation and the size of your store.
    -Advertise for possible employees.
    -Create a training program.
    -Hire and train new employees.

Using the list of five major components and establishing subsets of four or five components gives you specific items to focus on. Focusing your energy will provide greater results (see Focus). By mastering these five areas, your bookstore would have a much greater chance of succeeding.

Make a list of the five most important fundamentals in your area of interest. Then, list five important fundamentals for every goal. Now you know what it is you must do in order to succeed. Master these five things and certainly you will succeed.

Successful people have a knack for understanding and mastering the fundamentals in a given situation. They know that the little things are often the big things in any endeavor. People who take the time to learn the fundamentals will outperform those who underestimate the significance of fundamentals. Separate yourself from the crowd. Make sure you are a master of the fundamentals.

Give

The more he cast away the more he had.
- John Bunyan -Seventeenth century author of *Pilgrim's Progress*.

We often hear that it is better to give than to receive. In fact, I believe that you *must* give in order to receive. By giving your time and energy and money, you are sowing the seeds of the harvest that you will reap in the future. The benefits of involvement in organizations, working with people, and making contacts will come back to you many times over.

A young girl named Renee baby-sits to earn extra money. In stressing the importance of giving back to society, Renee's mother encouraged her to baby-sit free once a month. At first she didn't understand, and begrudgingly went along. The first time she baby-sat for free, the couple she worked for were caught off guard. The didn't know what to say. As time went on, Renee found that she enjoyed her free baby-sitting jobs more than the ones she was paid for. She prepared games and special projects for the nights that she gave away her services. It was very satisfying. One day the lady she baby-sat for gave Renee a beautiful shirt as a gift. Renee had not baby-sat for free because she expected something in return. In fact, the satisfaction she received from her generosity was far greater than any present she could have received. Nevertheless, she did greatly appreciate the shirt and it served to reinforce the value of giving back to the system.

Don't give back just because you expect something in return. Give because you believe that we can't just ask society to provide wonderful things for us without our being willing to give back in return. You will be pleased and amazed by the satisfaction you receive and the way your business and other primary desires are helped along by others.

Goals

People with goals succeed because they know where they are going.
- Earl Nightingale -Broadcaster, speaker, writer.

Goals are the targets derived from primary desires. In dealing with the gaps between our desires and achievements, we have an unyielding drive for growth and mastery, a creative mind, and a capacity for change. We have a desire to shape and build our own lives. It is important to try and master new skills. When we are children as young as 16-20 months we often shout *"me do, me do."* Naturally we don't set goals that are neither too demanding nor too easy. If they were too demanding, we would set ourselves up for failure. If they were too easy life would be boring. This level of effort is what psychologist Nicholas Hobbs calls *"the level of just manageable difficulty."* When we achieve our goals, it is only natural to reset them to a higher level of expectancy. Now we want to run faster, arrive sooner, achieve better results. It is in this manner that we grow.

A runner's muscles get sore after an intense workout. He must stretch and lengthen his muscles so that they can handle more and more stress. This process also allows the runner to run faster and faster. The soreness goes away after a few days, but the benefits remain. If we stretch our goals and continue to aim for higher and higher levels, we will have some soreness, but our capabilities will stretch and we will be able to obtain the higher goal.

Research shows that we are more apt to try a task if the risk of failure is about 50-50. Therefore, we should reduce our aversion to failure or place ourselves in a position to win. By reducing our aversion to failure, the fastest growth can be achieved. Traditional concepts of risk and reward apply in that, if we want something very much, we will be willing to accept more risk. In addition, if the reward of reaching our goals is great enough and we fully see and understand the rewards, we will not only be willing to risk less then desirable results but also we will be willing to sacrifice to achieve our goals.

Goals are the *"targets of life."* Greatness is impossible without goals. No commercial airplane ever took off without a predetermined destination. A ship never leaves its dock unless it is heading to a specific port. You must know what it is you desire before you can start achieving. Knowing is not enough, though. You must believe in your desires and you must understand the other principles outlined in this book so that you can achieve your goals. Not all goals need to be major goals. A successful life is filled with little successes as well as major ones.

You must constantly keep your goals in front of you, in your mind, in your eye. By doing so you, will always move towards the ultimate achievement of your goals. This will keep you from being sidetracked. It will keep you from giving in to activities and behaviors that are counterproductive to achieving the goals you have set. This, is willpower.

To make goals real put them in writing. By writing them down, you will be committing yourself to them. Your desires are just dreams until you write them down. Most people imagine things that they want but they are not willing to make the commitment of putting these goals on paper. They don't write down their goals because of fear (see Fear) or because they are not willing to put forth the work necessary to achieve their goals. You must decide, if you are a wisher or a worker.

Your goals should be as specific as possible. Vague goals give vague results. It is not enough to say "I want to be rich." What do you want your net worth to be? During what time period do you want to achieve this? In what trade or profession will you work? What percentage of your net worth will come from direct salary and what percentage from re-investment of earnings?

Develop a list of strategies that will help you reach your goal. The United States Army refers to this as METL, Mission Essentials Task List. By defining what it is you need to be doing on a monthly, weekly, daily and maybe even hourly basis, the big picture is broken down into smaller, more manageable parts. By reaching your hourly, daily, weekly, and monthly goals, your ultimate goal will be achieved in the process.

Your goals should be based only on your primary desires. Only through a high level of desire will you be able to commit to the work necessary to achieve your goals.

Remember, the areas in life for which you should set goals are:

Financial/Career	**Social**
Health	**Recreation**
Education	**Spiritual**
Family	

You must always aim high. Keep in mind however, that goals should build on one another. Each goal should be better than what you have previously attained. Your goals are the rungs on your ladder to success. As you achieve one goal, you will write another that will take you higher, and then higher. By setting and achieving smaller, short-term goals, you can experience success while maintaining a high level of motivation to move forward on the larger longer-term goals (see Motivation). Don't refuse to set high goals for fear that you will never reach them. You will work to the level of demand that you place on yourself (see Expectations).

Set your goals based on your perceptions of your skills. Many people underestimate their level of ability. It has been suggested that every individual is really three people: the person you think you are, the person others see you as, and the person you really are. Don't diminish your ability to take on a challenge. If you don't now possess all the skills necessary for the successful completion of a goal, you can pick them up along the way. We all have a great ability to learn new skills (see Skills).

Define your goals completely and comprehensively. Give yourself the targets you need to aim for. Your specific goals will fold into the details of your plan and be the benchmarks for the implementation phase of The Success Model.

Group

People seldom improve when they have no other model but themselves to copy after.
- Oliver Goldsmith -Eighteenth century British writer.

The key word "group" refers to the "master mind" principle that Napoleon Hill discusses in his book, *Think and Grow Rich*. The principle holds that we tend to like in others what we like in ourselves, and to dislike in others what we dislike in ourselves. Therefore, choose role models that you can learn from, people who have substance rather than appearance to offer. But do not compare yourself to others. Be successful in your own eyes. This group principle is that you can grow by being surrounded by individuals who have similar goals and desires. You can grow by being nourished by the strengths of others and vice versa.

Bring together a group of three to five people. Include people who work in different areas of business. This will provide you with a diverse base of knowledge. Set up regular meetings, perhaps a bi-monthly, luncheon meeting, in order to discuss specific topics. They may be current events or specific issues affecting someone at that time.

Members of the group should agree that information discussed at these meetings would be confidential. You will be amazed at the ideas that this group produces.

This work group will create for you an environment of successful people whose actions illustrate their success. It will also provide you an excellent sounding board for new ideas, a place to test your ideas, plans, and concepts. As you work on the primary desires in one of the areas of life, get advice from a successful group of people who are also actively working in that area. If, for example, you are working on your physical fitness desires, put together a group of people who are training or doing different types of exercise. Exchanging ideas will be very helpful.

Although input from others can be of great assistance, remember that only you know what you want and what you can do. Go with your instincts and move on your ideas and dreams. Use your success group to balance your thinking and help create ideas that will work for you. Your success group will bring different frames of reference to the table (see Paradigm) which will help open up possibilities as they relate to your desires. Your success group can and will have a large impact on your success journey.

Habits

Sow an act and you reap a habit.
Sow a habit and you reap a character.
Sow a character and you reap a destiny.
- Charles Reade -Nineteenth century British novelist.

Habits are personal attributes. You can have bad habits or good habits. The interesting thing about a bad habit is that if you change one, you usually get the good habit in return. You can lose a bad habit and pick up a good habit all through the same action. This phenomenon, which I call **Polar Habitude Transformation (PHT)**, is the act of eliminating a bad habit and gaining the resulting good habit in return. Polar habitude transformation will increase your drive to achieve your primary desires. PHT is the springboard of greatness. Eliminate bad habits, develop good habits, and move forward.

For example, if someone breaks the bad habit of telling lies, they becomes truthful. If someone stops the bad habit of procrastination, they becomes efficient. Eliminating a bad habit means you won't be held back by ill effects of the bad habit. You will move forward because of the good benefits of the newfound good habit. Successful people continually use PHT to achieve breakthroughs as they work on their primary desires.

An action must pertain to a ***primary desire*** in order to be successful at enhancing your good habits. Increasing the magnitude of good habits is a three step process.

1. List your good habits
2. Define in specific terms exactly what you need to do to maximize these habits.
3. On a daily basis, do what it is outlined in step 2 above.

In the window business, I decided I wanted to improve my follow-up in pursuing new business. I made the following list:

Send thank-you notes after all contacts.
Return phone calls within two hours.
Write quarterly update newsletters to my customers.

I worked very hard on these three items, thank-you notes, returning phone calls promptly, and putting together a four-page newsletter. The specific results of my efforts were hard to track. Then, one day a five-hundred-thousand-dollar customer told me that it was my persistence and follow-up that had won me the account. I felt rewarded, knowing my efforts had paid off.

What are the habits that might be keeping you from accomplishing your primary desires? To eliminate bad habits, you should:

1. Understand the negative characteristics of a bad habit.
2. Understand the positive characteristics of the good habit you will acquire when you eliminate a bad habit.
3. Define in specific terms exactly what you will need to do to change your behavior.
4. On a daily basis, do what you just decided needs to be done.

It is important to know what it is you don't like about a habit, so that you can move away from those traits. Once you are aware of what the negative habit is costing you, and not just in dollars, you will have an increased desire to change. Conversely, it is equally important to know what the traits are that you wish to attain. The reason *why* you want something is what brings about the results. It's the *reason* that you are changing that allows you to do it with passion and have the commitment, desire and energy necessary to see you through to achievement.

Perhaps you are aware of your bad habits. Let's say you habitually procrastinate and don't get goals completed on time. If you merely "think" that it would be nice to eliminate procrastination, that won't be good enough. You must be willing to *"walk through fire"* to eliminate this bad habit. In other words, is it or will it help you achieve a primary desire? If the answer is "yes," then you will be able to successfully apply the four steps listed above and get guaranteed results.

If you have determined that changing the negative behavior of procrastination relates to a primary desire, you must now understand the negative effect of procrastination.

What are you losing because of procrastination? Are you creating ill will? Are tasks not getting completed? What opportunities are you missing? What profits are you losing? Are you putting off investment decisions and fore-going higher returns on your money? Which relationships are going unfulfilled? What successes are you not enjoying? You could be missing out on a great deal of personal, social, and financial success because of the habit of procrastination.

Now, consider how you will benefit by changing pro-crastination to action. Will sending out thank-you's and fol-low-up letters generate more sales and higher earnings? Will taking certain steps help improve your relationships with a spouse, potential spouse, child, or friend? By finish-ing one project faster, will you have extra time to earn the extra money necessary to start your own business? There are so many potential gains from not procrastinating. What are your specific, potential gains?

Finally, you need to outline a plan of action. Maybe it's a commitment to write five thank-you's a day, call two friends an evening, or spend the time between dinner and eight o'clock with your children, reading books and playing games. The plan of action will vary based on individual pri-mary desires.

The main idea is that if you are working towards a primary desire, you will be willing to do the things neces-sary to obtain the end result. Go one step further and reward yourself on a regular basis for carrying out your action plan. This positive reward will encourage continued behavior modification.

By making the most of your good habits and eliminating your bad habits, you will be refining your personal
attributes and putting yourself in the best possible position
to maximize achievement.

Homework

Work is the meat of life, pleasure the dessert.
- Bertie Charles Forbes -Founder and publisher of *Forbes Magazine*.

Be prepared. You don't get paid for the performance, you get paid for the preparation.

Today, professional ball players earn millions of dollars each year. Are they getting paid for their performance for just that year? *No*. They get paid for all the years of hard work it took to get where they are. Many players started playing in Little League and high school before going to college where they played for four additional years. Then the players had to endure years of minor league play. There were all-night bus rides and cheap motels, and years of low pay. Once in the big leagues, they play for the league minimum salary. Only after years of training and work do these players earn the right to ask for big dollars. But when that time comes, they have the opportunity to earn millions.

When a boxer fights 15 rounds for a 20-million dollar

purse, he isn't getting paid for that night's work. He is being paid for the talent and skills and name recognition that it took years to develop. It's the same for you. If you want to be a good mother, you should read books on child rearing, such as *The Birth Order* by Dr. Kevin Leman. You should talk with other mothers who you feel are doing a good job. If you are seeking to excel in sales training, seminars would be invaluable homework as would reading books such as *How To Master The Art Of Selling* by Tom Hopkins. Someone wanting to improve his/her physical fitness level, should study nutrition, as well as exercise techniques. This homework will help you become the best possible at whatever you undertake.

Your actual performance is the combination of both your skill and the homework you have done to put you in a position to succeed. Seek that extra preparation. Look for ways that you can better yourself and your skill base. Expand your knowledge. You will be rewarded for the value you bring to the marketplace, and that value will be based largely on the homework you have done to better yourself. Do your homework!

Integrity

A single lie destroys a whole reputation of integrity.
- Baltasar Gracian -Spanish philosopher and writer.

People are said to have integrity when their actions are congruent with their values. To live with integrity you must have the strength to bridge the gap between your conscience and your conduct, between what you believe and what you do.

Integrity is a self-placed value, meaning, it is what you define it to be. Your integrity not only guides your actions but serves as an example for others. Integrity is tested when you are faced with a decision that may be advantageous to you but conflicts with your standard of ethics. Short-term gains must be ignored if you are to achieve the real long-term success you desire.

Universal laws make it impossible to act without integrity and to achieve total success, greatness, and happiness in the long-run. There may be short-term gains without integrity, but it is impossible to sustain long-term success. You may be able to make a great deal of money doing something illegal, but sooner or later you will be caught. If your business is morally wrong, you will not be able to share your successes with your family or friends.

Your associates and customers will see your integrity and act accordingly. If your customers see that you stick to what you believe in, then a greater sense of loyalty is formed. It will be harder for your competition to take away your customers. What is the example you are setting for your associates, employees, and friends? If your employees see you compromise your ethics, they will do the same because you have already shown that such behavior is acceptable. If co-workers see you act without integrity in your dealings with others, then they will have reason to question if you are acting with sincerity towards them.

Lack of integrity will weaken your position over time. Conversely, by acting with a high level of integrity, you set standards that those around you know they must live up to. Your actions will not only bring out the best in yourself but in others as well. You will find that long-term goals are much easier to achieve when you set the right examples and apply a high level of integrity to your life.

Internalization

You are today where your thoughts have brought you; you will be tomorrow where your thoughts take you.
- James Allen -Nineteenth century American novelist.

Internalization separates the true super achiever or champion from the also-ran. True super achievers will see themselves already owning the results of their goals. They see themselves going through the steps necessary to reach their goals. They see themselves attaining the pinnacle. Just as world class runners win the race in their mind, super achievers imagine implementing their plans and see themselves achieving their goal. They condition their mind for success.

John Smoltz, starting pitcher for the Atlanta Braves, was 5-0 in his first five decisions during playoff and World Series games in 1991 and 1992. "I do relish it," he said. "It's fulfilling a dream. I've probably pitched in one thousand of these games as a kid, imagining I'm in the playoffs."

By replaying in your mind a perfect execution of a set of plans for an athletic event, you are actually preparing yourself for the big day. Before ice skaters step onto the ice for a big performance, they rehearse their performance in their mind. Doing so reinforces the performance and puts the mind in a position of just having to repeat this rehearsed performance on the ice. The mind cannot distinguish what is real and what is being programmed. In other words, your mind cannot differentiate between the positive results of an actual experience and the desired results of a vividly imagined experience. If you are in sales, you should rehearse a presentation in your mind before you make it. Before you have that conversation with your child, rehearse it in your mind. Imagine how you want the meeting with your boss to go. See yourself achieving the results you desire. Now, when it comes time for the real thing, you have prepared *and* rehearsed. Who will be more successful, the person trying for the first time or the person who has rehearsed many times before the big event?

In 1959, during the Cultural Revolution in China, Liu Chi Kung, a master concert pianist, was imprisoned. For seven straight years Liu was denied the use of a piano. Shortly after he was released, however, Liu was back on tour. The critics gave him rave reviews! When questioned on how he was able to perform so well without having the benefit of practice for seven years, Liu replied: "I did practice. Every day I rehearsed every piece I ever played, note by note, in my mind."

The old expression *"practice makes perfect"* is only partially true. Perfect practice makes perfect performance. What if every time you practiced a song on the piano you played it wrong? Even if you practiced the song a hundred times, as long as you practiced it incorrectly, you would never play it correctly. Professional athletes stop practicing their sport when they get tired. They know that when they are tired, they pick up bad habits that will then affect their performance. Make sure that when you practice you practice correctly.

By reviewing over and over in your mind all the steps necessary to achieve what it is you would like to achieve, you are rehearsing. You are preparing for the perfect sales presentation. You are ready for that talk with your boss or family member. You are ready to implement the steps necessary to reach your goal. Visualization techniques should be practiced and refined. First, you must internalize your goals and practice your presentations in your mind. Then, you will be ready to implement them in the real world.

Knowledge

If a man empties his purse into his head, no man can take it away from him. An investment in knowledge always pays the best interest.
- Benjamin Franklin -American writer, scientist and printer.

Without the proper knowledge and education in a specific field, you cannot become the very best. It is difficult, if not impossible, to achieve in an area unless you are educated in that field. Very often, people resist learning because it implies they don't know something. It also means starting at the bottom, which means risking failure or embarrassment because you are not knowledgeable about a specific topic. True achievers must overcome this fear. True achievers learn new things and study new topics so that they can continue to grow in their field of choice and in order to balance their education.

When embarking on the learning adventure you must first conquer the basics. Findings demonstrate that, because it reduces energy demands on the brain, practicing simple things makes the acquisition of later information more efficient.

It is important to be a well-rounded person. A well-rounded person is interesting company. And by being interesting, you will be able to increase your exposure to various groups of people. People like to be with interesting, educated people. You will be included in the right groups. You will be surrounding yourself with the right people. You will be making the right connections. You will be forming the right relationships. These relationships will help you learn more and help you achieve your primary desires.

I know a woman who took a poetry course at a nearby college. She enjoyed it and begin to take more courses. By expanding her education this way she became a more interesting person. Travel is another great way to expand your education. For years my father traveled around the world twice a year on business. In addition, he and my mother make it a point to vacation in different countries whenever they can. Their exposure to different people and cultures has been phenomenal. They are both very interesting people and have given many presentations on the countries they have visited. This knowledge base infiltrates everything they do. My father's sales ability is enhanced through his ability to effectively communicate with a broader base of people. Remember, communication is a key to success, and a broad-based education will improve your ability to communicate and will widen the base of people with whom you can communicate.

Being able to converse about subjects that others are interested in, you show that you care about who they are, what they do, and what they believe in. This enables you to solicit their help when you need assistance and enhance the achievement of your primary desires. As you learn more and communicate better, you will be included by more people. This will give you the opportunity to learn from an even broader base. Imagine how much faster you can achieve your primary desires if you can communicate effectively with peers at work, your boss, employees, children, your spouse or even your neighbors.

Continuing education is the process that begins when your formal education (high school, college, etc.) ends. I also use the term "continuing" because, for real achievers, the education process never ends. Continuing education is driven by commitment. Since you will be studying and learning what is necessary to achieve your primary desires you will have the energy, commitment, and enthusiasm necessary to acquire that information. You will do this because you know that the information you come away with will give you the personal confidence and the necessary tools to achieve your primary desires, the desires for which you are willing to "walk through fire." As a matter of fact, when you are learning information pertaining to your primary desire, you will enjoy gaining this new knowledge. You will enjoy reading the books. You will enjoy the classes, tapes and seminars.

My 9-year old son loves to read children adventure stories. He is interested in other children his age and enjoys reading about their exploits. He can read for hours! But he would not be able to read very long about economics or physics. He just does not have a primary desire to learn about those topics. Always study and learn about areas that you enjoy or pertain to your primary desires.

Sometimes you may have to study something that

you find uninteresting or boring, although the information is critical to your ultimate success. An example might be having to study bookkeeping in order to be able to accurately keep track of necessary information for your retail store. The desire to operate a profitable store must be strong enough to keep you committed to your education even when the specific subject is not your primary interest.

No one is born with the skills to do everything. They must be taught. Babies cannot read, or talk, or walk, or use a fork and spoon. They must be taught all these skills. They must learn these things just as later in life they need to learn how to sell or how to be a good parent or spouse. What people **are** born with is the ability to gain knowledge. If we can learn the techniques of achievement, we can reach for and obtain greatness. Some people stop their formal education when they leave school. This is a mistake. The real achiever is always reading books, watching videos, and listening to cassettes. The real achiever is always gaining knowledge.

Many professionals are *required* to put in a certain number of hours or to attend a certain number of classes annually in order to maintain their license. Doctors, lawyers and accountants, for example, are required to broaden their education base. Would you want to go to a doctor who was still practicing the techniques used in the 60's? Several years ago I had a knee injury that required arthroscopic surgery. I had the surgery on Friday morning and was walking that afternoon. By Tuesday, I was riding a bicycle. Seven weeks later, I ran a marathon! If this had happened ten years earlier I would have had to have major knee surgery and my leg would have been in a cast for three months followed by three months of rehabilitation. What a difference it made because the medical field had progressed and my doctor continued his education.

Drive time is my favorite time to listen to educational or motivational tapes. That way, I am doing two things at once and making the most of my time. Successful people say that when they stop learning they feel "dead." The world is constantly changing and what worked last year might not work tomorrow. You must always be honing your skills.

One of life's best teachers is experience. Always ask yourself, "What can I learn from this situation?" Time is limited and you can only have so many experiences in a day, a week, or a year. However, you also learn from the experiences of others. By reading (biographies, autobiographies, and relevant magazines,) and having discussions (with a mentor, other successful people, or members of your success group), you will be able to expand your experience base geometrically. What a powerful source of knowledge! (see Mentor.)

We discussed the value of reading. Instructional audio and videotapes are also a tremendous source of information. In addition, seminars, conferences, and courses should be a part of your educational plan.

Before getting into public speaking, I went to The Dale Carnegie Center of Excellence where I received private tutoring on effective speaking for all types of situations. I worked on speeches, interviews, and training techniques. This training was invaluable and the knowledge helped me grow as a speaker at a much more accelerated rate than if I had plodded along on my own.

Tapes, books, seminars and other educational methods are fine, but if you don't internalize and apply the knowledge to your primary desires, you might as well spend your time doing something else. *It's not just what you know, but what you do with what you know.*

"*GIGO*" is a term used in computer information systems. It stands for "garbage in, garbage out." A computer can only do what you tell it to do. If you input the right information, it will provide you the proper output. But if you give erroneous instructions, you will get erroneous results. Your brain is a fantastic computer. Give it the best instructions and information available, and it will provide you with terrific results. Develop your skills until you become the best in your chosen field. Get all the knowledge you can!

Leadership

The final test of a leader is that he leaves behind him in other men the conviction and the will to carry on.
- Walter Lippmann -Twentieth century journalist and Pulitzer Prize winner.

A good leader is able to motivate other people to perform at or above their previous best in order to produce results that will help the leader achieve his primary desires. A true leader helps others think about themselves rather than thinking about the leader. A true leader can help others succeed and thereby help himself to succeed. If you help people get what they want, then they will help you get what you want. Sometimes you can give a little and receive much in return. Of course, you need to know what it is that someone wants or needs.

A leader's basic responsibility is to build a team whereby individual strengths are enhanced and weaknesses are reduced to insignificant levels. A good leader has the ability to develop mutual respect and motivate those around him/her. A good leader provides vision and direction for the team.

In a recent popular Hollywood movie, a look-alike is hired to impersonate the President of The United States. At first, he takes his job lightly and only does it for the money. Shortly after he starts, he asks a Secret Service Agent if he would sacrifice his life for the president and actually shield the President from gun fire. The Agent did not respond. He did not want anything to do with the impersonator. When the real President dies unexpectedly, the look-alike assumes the presidency and begins putting the good of the people before conventional politics and himself. The presidential look-alike helps the homeless and shows compassion for all people. After exposing several corrupt officials, he loses the job as "president." Before he walks off to disappear into the crowd, the same Secret Service Agent turns to him and says: "I'd take a bullet for you." This kind of loyalty is the result of his having exhibited great leadership qualities. He makes people feel appreciated. He puts their good above his own short term gains.

Developing good leadership qualities will enable you to motivate others and gain their assistance in your conquest of barriers as you move to achieve your primary desires.

Life

I think that, as life is action and passion, it is required of a man that he should share the passion and action of his time at peril of being judged not to have lived.
- Oliver Wendell Holmes -Nineteenth century physician, writer.

Life is not made up of things but of experiences. A mentor once told me that it is not the things that you buy that you will remember, but the times that you share and the places you go that you will always carry with you. Think back on your life. What are your most fond memories? Do you recall things that you have bought or times you shared with someone and places you visited?

I enjoy listening to music and several years ago, I purchased a complete stereo system. I bought two amplifiers, four speakers, a pre-amplifier, compact disc player, tape recorder, and a stereo video recorder. The system had Dolby Surround Sound capability and sounded fantastic! But I can honestly say that I never reminisce about times I spend in the family room listening to music. However, when Renee was pregnant with our first child, Geoffrey, we took an inexpensive trip to a resort in mid-Missouri. The weather was cold for the first week of June, but we had a blast. We had just moved to St. Louis from Atlanta and the four days we spent together were very special. We always smile when we think back to that trip.

One summer, Renee and I took a two-week trip to Europe. We happened to be in Paris during the French Open tennis tournament. I was able to obtain two tickets for a day at Roland Garros, where the French Open is played. The tickets cost more than a night's stay at the finest hotel in Paris. We spent the entire day moving from court to court watching our favorite tennis players. Between matches, we drank bottled water and ate great French bread. If you ask Renee about that trip, she cannot recall anything she purchased, but we both agree the highlight of the entire trip was the day we shared at Roland Garros.

The most fulfilled lives have frequent and varied experiences. Fill your experiences with emotion and energy. Give them your "all." This will maximize your experiences and make them even more memorable. Live your life with tremendous passion (see Passion).

What is the quality of your life today? Is it different than yesterday? Do you want it to be different tomorrow? Are you where you envisioned yourself? You can use The Success Model to achieve great things if you apply the techniques in your life. Don't leave anything to chance. Create the life you deserve and have the experiences that will make it memorable.

Listen

If I listen, I have the advantage; if I speak, others have it.
- From the Arabic

The average person spends over 70% of his/her life in an awakened state. During this time, you are constantly communicating either with yourself or with others. Good communication skills are critical to success. People judge you by your ability to effectively convey your thoughts. There are four main modes of communication: reading, speaking, writing, and listening. Reading, speaking and writing are part of the school curriculum from grade school through high school. For the most part, few people have had any formal education in listening. However, effective listening skills are crucial to your success.

One time a customer came into my office to discuss our quality control. He expressed that his company was important to him and that he had to do whatever necessary to make it grow. What he really said was: "Get it right or I'm going to take my business elsewhere." I made the mistake of not hearing him and almost lost the account. Only some quick work saved a one-hundred-thousand-dollar customer, a customer that always paid his bills on time!

It is important to listen not only to what people say but to what they mean. Interpret the feelings they are expressing. People want to be appreciated. Fulfill their want by listening to them: it shows that you care.

People have difficulty listening because of bad habits they have developed over time. One bad habit is talking. It is impossible to listen if you are talking. However, unfortunately, most people feel that as long as they are speaking they are in control. Actually, the opposite may be true. Only through listening can we learn. We have two ears and one mouth. Use them in that ratio and you will become an excellent listener.

Listen not only to the words but to how they are delivered. Meaning is in people and not just in their words. Listen for the *intent*, not just the content. Pay attention to changes in pace. Listen for voice inflections. Look "between the lines" for the real meaning. This is all called listening empathetically. You care, not just about what someone says, but why they say it. It is this greater understanding that will enable you to form the correct response to a particular situation and ultimately get the results from the relationship you desire.

If during a conversation you are showing that you are actively listening and are interested in what is being said, the speaker will give you more information. This is how your knowledge and resulting power grows. There are several ways to enhance your listening skills and to show that you are interested in the person speaking to you. I have created a technique called *FRAG*, which is short for "fragment." A fragment is a piece or part of a whole; something is missing. Likewise, if you don't use good listening skills, you will only receive part of the message. Your response to an individual will be limited. In addition, having only partial information may leave you in a less competitive position. FRAG stands for:

Finish
Rephrase and repeat
Ask questions
Gestures

First, always let the speaker finish his/her comments. Don't interrupt and don't change the subject. This assures you of receiving the complete message. Also, it is polite!

Second, repeat a portion of what the speaker said. This shows that you listened and understood the speaker. Rephrase the statement in your own words. By rephrasing and repeating what the speaker said, you will be sure that you understand the message and you will also show that you are both interested and sincere.

Third, ask questions. This, too, shows that you are interested. And it encourages the speaker to continue and expand on his/her message providing more valuable information. By asking questions, you can ask the person for clarification of the message for exact meaning, thus insuring understanding of the communication.

Fourth, use simple gestures such as a frown, eye contact, a smile, or a nod to signal that you are involved in the conversation. This sends positive feedback to the speaker and helps you maintain your concentration and interest.

By using the **FRAG** technique, you will receive the entire message and not just fragments. At the same time, you will develop a good rapport with the speaker.

It has been said that information is power. With good listening skills, you can obtain more information and have greater power. As your listening skills improve, you will get more out of each conversation, while at the same time, earning the respect of the person speaking to you. A positive relationship is based on effective, *two-way* communication. Listening is an essential part of good communication.

Little

Order and simplification are the first steps toward the mastery of a subject...
- Thomas Mann -Twentieth century German writer and Nobel Prize winner.

It's the little things that count. Too often, people only think about the big picture. High achievers have the ability to isolate the little, but important, elements of a task and concentrate on them. Working on the basics is one technique that makes them successful.

Pick out the four or five little things that can separate you from the pack and do them better than anyone else. You will succeed while others are on the sidelines watching. It is these little differences that set you apart, put you ahead, and help you achieve. If you do the little things well, many times the big things will fall into place on their own.

I service my car at a dealer who has found that it's the little things that make his service first-class. When I drop off my car, the service representative offers to drive me to work or to pay for a taxi. They always call me when the job is done or provide a free loaner car if they take longer than it was estimated to perform the service. Finally, I get a call five to seven days after the service to make sure the job was done to my satisfaction. By doing the little things well, and focusing on my needs, they are able to do a superior job and insure that they have me as a satisfied customer.

In *Golf Digest* every month, they feature the top golf professionals and their salaries to date. In addition, they compare the number of strokes separating the number one money maker from the number two player. The difference per round may be as little as .35 strokes, yet the difference in average earnings may be as much as $35,000 per tournament. Isolating and working on the subtleties of the game may only take a fraction of a point off of a professional golfer's score, but it could add up to a significant amount of money over the course of a full season.

Renee has a list of several girls she uses as baby-sitters. One girl, Allison, does a great job of cleaning up the toys that our children play with. Additionally, if Allison feeds the children dinner, she always cleans up nicely. Given a choice, which baby-sitter do you think Renee is going to hire? It is the extra effort that Allison puts forth on the "little things" that insures her job security.

Sometimes, people look for shortcuts in life, which usually means they end up with average results. The real achiever knows that it is the little things that add up to **big** results. Real achievers make the effort. They isolate the little things and focus on them. This sets them apart from the competition. Real achievers master the little things.

Luck

Chance favors the prepared mind.
- Louis Pasteur -Nineteenth century French chemist.

Some people look at other successful people and make excuses for their achievements. A popular excuse is, "He's just lucky." There is no such thing as naked luck. Luck is when you are prepared to take advantage of the opportunities that naturally present themselves. Don't confuse luck with hard work and preparation. Throughout life, there will be many chances to get ahead. It's your responsibility to be in a position to take advantage of those opportunities. As you increase your knowledge, education, and skills, you increase your preparedness. As you increase your preparedness, you will be able to take advantage of an increasing number of opportunities. When that happens you can begin to pick and choose the best opportunities. You can seek out the best results with the highest probability of success!

Robert Shaw, CEO of International Jensen, Inc., a $153 million manufacturer of home and automobile speakers, went to Japan to solicit business from the Mazda Motor Corporation. After lengthy meetings on Friday, Shaw was told that if he wanted to submit a bid on upcoming work, it would have to be submitted by Monday, and it had to be in Japanese. Shaw had three days. Shaw's team worked through the weekend and, on Sunday, submitted their bid before leaving Japan. It turned out to be the winning bid and the beginning of a long relationship with Mazda. The chance to bid had nothing to do with luck: it was the outcome of Shaw's careful preparation of nearly six months. International Jensen learned from their relationship with Mazda and expanded their exports. This was all possible because Shaw was prepared for the opportunity when it presented itself.

My window company spent several years developing a comprehensive marketing program for our dealers. Our color brochures were the finest in the industry. We offered training manuals for dealers to use with their sales force. We provided direct mail literature. We put together a whole assortment of window samples and display cases of window parts. In other words, we offered the dealer a chance to really impress the homeowner customer. Because of this complete marketing program, we won several large accounts. Obviously, it hadn't been luck that brought us these large accounts. It was because we were well-prepared and added value to our customers which created opportunities.

Another popular excuse for dismissing the success of others is, "Oh, she's a born winner." I don't believe in the notion of a "born winner." Success is based on skills not genes. I seriously doubt that in the delivery room, right after the birth of a baby, the attending surgeon said, "Now there's a born winner." Winning is the result of good input, such as good research or good advice, and hard work. If you buy into the notion that there are no born winners, then you must also buy into the notion that there are no "born losers."

Take this a little further. If there are no born losers, then everyone can be a winner, if they have the right input and apply themselves in a positive manner. The beautiful part of all this is that there is no time limit on when the quality input must occur. You can benefit from quality input just as well if it comes in your 50's as if it had come in your teens. As a matter of fact, later in life you may be in a better position to take immediate action on the road to success.

You can make your own *luck* through diligent and thorough preparation. If you take advantage of the opportunities that naturally present themselves other people might think that **you are the born winner.**

Mentor

No man is so foolish but he may sometimes give another good counsel, and no man so wise that he may not easily err if he takes no other counsel than his own. He that is taught only by himself has a fool for a master.
- Ben Jonson -Sixteenth century English dramatist.

It is difficult to improve yourself if your own set of skills is the only model you have to follow. To reach a higher level of skills and abilities you must strive for them; but before you can strive for them, you must be able to see them in others. See those skills and abilities in others first, then, adapt and apply them to yourself.

Someone who is a good role model performs two functions.

1) He/she provides a good example of what you want to be.

2) He/she provides an excellent source of information and knowledge.

People who have achieved a high level of success will encourage others to go out and achieve similar success. Take advice from people who have achieved what you want to achieve and who possess the qualities and traits of the successful person that you want to attain. Someone who has worked for a wage all his life, will be unlikely to advise you on starting your own business. People who have never achieved high levels of success will be hesitant to tell you to take a chance and work toward your primary desires.

Successful people are willing to share their successes with those who show ambition. Don't hesitate to approach someone who is successful in your field. They will take your interest as a compliment. Additionally, you can shorten the learning curve and time needed for success by taking their advice. You can attain important knowledge from books, but wise men and women give practical advice based on their experiences. You can learn from the mistakes of others without having to make the same mistakes yourself. This is an extremely important concept to adopt.

I have been very fortunate to have been taught by two of the greatest salespeople I know, my father, Rubin, and Tom Hopkins. After graduating from graduate school, I went into sales. I trained with my father for two weeks. It was time to go on my own and I adopted the strategy of just trying to imitate what my father did. I knew that if I was only 50% as good at using the techniques as my father I would be considered successful. After time, I could add my own embellishments to the system. This plan worked for me and in a matter of months, I was the number one salesperson on a team of twelve. In a short time, I was able to outsell the next best representative by about two to one.

One of the secrets to success is to emulate the best to get immediate and great results. Then, and only then improve the system to become a superstar.

Later in my selling career, I was introduced to Tom Hopkins. Tom has successfully trained over one million salespeople. Tom is a stickler for details. He helped me refine my selling skills by teaching me to pay attention to details. It is the little things that can make, or possibly kill, a sale. Just using one wrong word in your closing sequence can blow the entire opportunity. Tom also taught the value of scripting out specific closes for any situation. By writing out closes that are tailored to your particular industry, and then rehearsing them until they become second nature, you are prepared for almost anything the customer can throw at you.

After almost two years of rapport building with an account in Chicago I was in a position to close on a window program that would amount to over four-hundred-thousand-dollars a year. I felt that the main obstacle to my success would be thirty-thousand-dollars of service credits the dealer was earning as rebates from his existing supplier. I structured my pricing so I would be able to offer year-end rebates that more than offset my client's lost credits from his former supplier. By preparing a specific close for his possible objection, I was in position when the concern was raised by my client, to handle the objection and make the sale.

Major corporations such as Xerox Corporation use a powerful technique called "benchmarking." Benchmarking allows you to gain the most from your mentor relationships. It has become an important part of many Total Quality

Management programs in recent years. Xerox perfected the techniques in the 1970's and used them to successfully beat back Japanese competitors producing cheaper copiers.

Benchmarking is made up of four parts:

- Identify areas that need improvement.
- Search out examples of other companies or individuals that excel in your area of interest.
- Study the techniques used by those companies and individuals to achieve the "best in their field" status that they enjoy.
- Apply those same techniques in order to achieve significant improvements in your own performance.

If you were starting a new company and felt that in addition to your industry knowledge and good buying skills you needed improvement in internal accounting controls and marketing, you could use benchmarking to accelerate your success. Seek out someone who exhibits excellent knowledge and use of accounting, statistics, and controls in his/her company. Then, find someone else who has a great track record in marketing and product promotion. Now, speak with these people and learn from them. By carefully defining the areas where you need help and by "target benchmarking," you will get a higher level of quality information to apply to your business.

The best benchmark projects are those that have specific, well defined, and narrowly focused objectives. Don't try to analyze the big picture. Work on specific elements of your plan. Most of all, implement the information you obtain. Many times people work hard to make the right connections, obtain valuable information and then do nothing with it.

I continue to seek out advice from experts in any field in which I wish to excel. If I am interested in a something, I am only interested in excelling at it. Mentors will make the difference in your performance. Making and learning from your own mistakes is often too costly, both in time and money. Find people who will share their experiences and knowledge with you. This will greatly shorten the time it takes to achieve your primary desires.

Momentum

Give yourself something to work toward - constantly.
- Mary Kay Ash -Founder of Mary Kay Cosmetics.

To start or learn something new, we must stop what we are currently doing. This takes more effort than most of us are willing to put forth.

I bought a pinball game for my children. At first, they were concerned about how difficult the machine was. Then, my daughter did well during one of her turns. All of a sudden her interest in the game zoomed! People naturally avoid failure. As a result, a small success can turn into instant enthusiasm and a desire to try again. A small success accomplished early on in any endeavor can build interest, commitment, and momentum. Therefore, many people provide an opportunity to achieve a small success early on in their plans. Use momentum to your advantage and let it help you get over any hurdles you may face.

Many times I hear about a successful company and someone says, "That company came out of nowhere." What really happened was the company put in many years of hard work building positive momentum. Their products were in place. Their support staff was in place. Their promotion was in place. With all this positive momentum built up the "lid" blew off and the company was able to enjoy the fruits of their patience and labors. Momentum can be a strong force.

Since others around you are always moving, it is impossible for you to remain in the same place. You either move up or move down. You have a choice. Make the decision to have *forward* momentum.

Motivation

As long as I have a want, I have a reason for living. Satisfaction is death.
- George Bernard Shaw -Twentieth century Irish-born British playwright.

There are two types of motivation, extrinsic and intrinsic. Extrinsic motivation comes from people around you. Many people attend a motivational seminar and leave "all pumped up." This is an example of extrinsic motivation. This type of motivation is short lived. If you don't internalize the motivation so that it comes from within, then the momentary "high" will disappear and you will not change your direction or behavior. It's impossible for extrinsic motivation to become internalized unless it relates directly to a primary desire. By internalizing motivation, so that it is *you* that becomes the driving force in your life, you will be in a position to maintain the energy necessary to progress toward your primary desires.

Wood, a traditional building material in our society, has been replaced in many products by high-tech plastics. Polyvinyl chloride (PVC), a type of plastic, has an interesting characteristic compared to wood. When wood is ignited, it will burn until there is nothing left. PVC, on the other hand, will not sustain a flame. In other words, if a burning match is held next to the PVC it will burn, but when the match is removed, the flame on the PVC will go out. Wood, however, will continue to burn after the match is removed. Are you wood or plastic? *How deep is your motivation?* If you go to a seminar or attend a sales meeting and have a healthy dose of motivation, is it internalized? How long does it last? Is it gone the next day, or are you able to sustain the high level of motivation and exert a high level of activity? This high level of activity will enable you to accomplish the many steps necessary to fully implement your plan and achieve your goals. Only your primary desires are powerful enough to generate and sustain the motivation necessary for valuable goal-setting and ultimate achievement.

Successful people set goals that are slightly above their previous best effort. In reaching these goals, they grow in skill and stature and fuel the fire of motivation. It is important to devise a system that will provide measurable successes on a daily and weekly basis. As long as you can see yourself moving towards the achievement of another meaningful goal, you will stay motivated (see Goals).

Intrinsic motivation will provide the strongest push toward your primary desires. Be like wood. Sustain your own fire in order to always maintain forward momentum toward your primary desires.

Now

Every body continues in its state of rest, or of uniform motion in a right line, unless it is compelled to change that state by forces impressed upon it.
- Sir Isaac Newton -Seventeenth century mathematician and philosopher.

Get it started now! The past is a bucket of ashes. The future is yet to unfold. The only moment of time we can control is now. Now is the time to start on your new program. Most people never get going, even when they know what it is they need to do. "I'll start tomorrow," they say. Tomorrow never comes and they never get started. If you don't start today, why would you start tomorrow? The only way to guarantee success is to begin. And the time to begin is *now*!

Older people often lament, "If I were young again, I would . . . ." Then, they fill in the blank with all kinds of great things. They regret the opportunities they didn't take. They regret the "nows" that got away.

A Rabbi once told me of a man that put off visiting a relative. The man lived in a different town and always said,

"I'll go visit her next month." Well a bunch of "next months" came and went and one day he received a call that she had died. How do you think he felt? I would almost bet that his exact words were, "If I had only gone to see her . . ." *If it is important do it now!*

Don't put off determining what your primary desires are. Don't put off committing to change. Don't put off creating and implementing your plans. Don't ignore the opportunities to grow and become what it is you really want to become. Don't put off your mission of fulfilling your destiny.

In March, 1991, Orestes Lorenzo, a Cuban pilot, flew his MiG-23 to the Key West naval air station in Florida. He had defected to the United States and in the process, left behind his wife and two small sons. Within three months, Orestes had obtained visas for his wife and children. Although the Cuban government had stated many times that anybody with visas from another country would be free to leave, they would not let Orestes' family leave Cuba. Orestes conducted a hunger strike, used short-wave radio broadcasts to Havana in an attempt to embarrass Castro, and even contacted Soviet leader Mikhail Gorbachev. Finally he planned a more direct approach. He flew to Cuba below radar, in a Cessna twin-engine airplane, landed on a quiet road and flew out with his family. Had he been caught, the penalty would have been death. *Readers Digest* quoted a note written by Orestes before leaving on his dramatic flight. The note said: "Those who fail do so because they wait for things to happen. Those who succeed do so because they make things happen."

Pretend for a minute that you can accurately see into the future and you know without a shadow of a doubt that you will be successful in your primary desire that pertains to finances. By seeing into the future, you know that your first company will go bankrupt. You will have to mortgage your home to finance your second company which will be on the verge of bankruptcy before things turn around after two years. In your third year of business you will earn $200,000.00. Knowing these temporary setbacks, when would you start your company? Most people would say, "Right now!" Well, you may not know the time frame for your success, but if you define your primary desires and apply them to The Success Model with the energy, enthusiasm, and the kind of commitment that only a primary desire can generate, you will be successful. You have to be, because the desire will be so great that you will find a way, no matter how long it takes. The stronger the desire, the harder you will apply yourself, and the faster you will be able to achieve your goal.

Opportunity

Do not wait for extraordinary circumstances to do good; try to use ordinary situations.
- Jean Paul Richter -Nineteenth century German writer.

Non-achievers will wait for opportunity to knock at their door. This will not happen, because opportunity is within *you*! You must make opportunity happen. Discover what it is you want in your life. Calculate the price, and then pay it. It's just like shopping. When you select a new suit or television, you look at the price tag. If you still want the television, you simply pay the amount of money necessary to get it. Define your primary desires. What changes will you have to commit to? What sacrifices will you have to make to successfully implement your plan? What is the price you will have to pay to enjoy the rewards of your primary desires?

By relying on yourself instead of others, you are relying on the one person over whom you have control. You can control your thoughts, your ambitions, your goals, your planning, and your time. You can count on yourself to come through when it is necessary.

Living in the United States affords everyone wonderful opportunities. People have come here from all over the world, with little or no money, and made a great success of themselves. There are no guarantees in life, there are only opportunities. Take advantage of your opportunities.

Paradigm

Never, never rest contented with any circle of ideas, but always be certain that a wider one is still possible.

- Richard Jefferies -Nineteenth century English naturalist and novelist.

An individual's paradigms are the set of rules by which they *think* the game of life is played. Your paradigms dictate the way you see the world around you. You can have major improvements in your life by shifting your reference points. Since your paradigms are the basis of your reference points, a change in your paradigms will ultimately affect the greatest change in your life.

Paradigms are a result of the environment that you grew up in as well as your current environment and social surrounding. Your self-image is formed as you develop in life (see Self-image). Your paradigms are affected by your self-image with respect to your capabilities. Your environment will shape your paradigms in conjunction with the world around you. To be able to have a paradigm shift, which is what is necessary to have a remarkable change in achievement and success in your life, you must be open to those changes. Herein is where the difficulty lies: unless you have strong self-esteem it will be difficult to open your-self up to these changes in reference and belief. If you have a poor self-image, you will be more concerned with protecting your current position by sticking with the status quo. It is hard to open up to change if you are busy protecting what you have. By working on your self-esteem and self-image, you will essentially put yourself in a position to shed the chains holding you back. You will be able to open up your mind to new ideas so that you can achieve a paradigm shift and be in a position for significant success in your life.

In 1952, The Lipton Tea Company invented the flo-thru tea bag. People around the world see tea bags as being rectangular in shape and attached by a string to a paper tag. Forty years later Tetley Tea made a paradigm shift. They decided "tea bags can be different. Tea cups are round. Saucers are round. Why not have round tea bags?" After introducing the new product in England, Tetley's sales increased over 40%, becoming number-one in the market! The round tea bag has now been released in Canada and the United States, with similar success.

When I first entered the window business our customer base included medium and small window retailers. Larger retailers purchased their windows out of town because they had the purchasing volume to justify shipments. The retailers believed that by marketing an *exclusive* window, they could get a higher price than for a window that was available elsewhere. The small and medium retailers did not have access to the same product, so if home-owners wanted the *exact* window the large company showed them, they had to pay the price the large retailer was asking. My experience for the first two years in the window business was that a local manufacturer could not successfully sell a large in-town account. One day, I had a paradigm shift. I decided that *anyone* could create an exclusive product. The fact that my factory was located in the same market as the large dealer did not matter. Once I realized that I could offer something different, I set out to create our exclusive window. I had not tried before, because my paradigm had dictated that exclusivity did not exist for me. After only a short time, I came up with a program of exclusive product features and unique marketing ideas. Our first large account bought half a million dollars worth of windows on an annual basis. The second account spent over two million dollars with us annually! My original paradigm was shaped by the people I worked with. Look at the success I was able to achieve by changing my reference points. This paradigm shift was worth over fifty-thousand-dollars in annual commissions and worth far more to the company in profits and increased buying power.

Some time ago, we decided to expand our product line with an additional high quality vinyl window. Everyone in the industry felt that a top quality replacement window had to be fusion welded at the joints. Fusion welding is labor intensive and requires expensive welding and cleaning equipment. I started researching other manufacturing methods and began evaluating different options. Finally, we found a method of fastening that was 30% stronger than welding. It didn't involve expensive manufacturing equipment, so we were able to tool up for half the cost of a traditional welded system. Even better, we were able to reduce our labor costs by approximately one-third! We became more competitive and sales of this new product skyrocketed. These drastic results were all possible because of our paradigm shift: because we had changed our view on how quality windows had to be manufactured.

Evaluate your paradigms. By shifting your points of reference, can you open up new areas of potential growth? Don't say, "that's impossible." Say, "how can I make that possible?" Things that were not possible before will become possible. Your ability to achieve will be enhanced and the time needed to achieve your primary desires will be reduced.

Passion

A strong passion for any object will ensure success, for the desire of the end will point out the means.
- William Hazlitt -Eighteenth century British essayist.

Perhaps the most important key word is passion. It is passion that fuels desire and desire that starts The Success Model. Passion is the seed of all success. It is the foundation for every accomplishment. Passion is the source, the fountain of youth, or at least the energy of continued youth. Passion is the energy that it takes to implement The Success Model, achieve your goals and enjoy success.

Your level of passion will dictate your level of success. You must apply passion in each step of The Success Model. Use passion in determining your primary desires. Use passion in committing to the changes necessary in your life to do the things that will let you enjoy success. Use passion when writing out your goals. As you see in your mind's eye what it is you want and how you will feel when you accomplish your goals, let the passion flow through your veins. Let your passion drive your creativity when designing the plans necessary to accomplish your goals.

Then, when you implement your plan, fill each step with your strongest passion as to insure the highest degree of effort at each stage.

I know a very good piano teacher who gives her students pencils as incentives for small accomplishments like practicing a certain amount of time or mastering a new song. The pencils have musical symbols printed on them and are inexpensive, but they provide great motivation to her students. At a recent recital, all the students were given a trophy to signify outstanding achievement. You should have seen the pride and excitement on their faces! Before the trophies were handed out, the teacher told the audience: "Outside of my family, piano and teaching piano are my true passions in life." That really summed it up. Her passion is evident in her actions. Her passion results in tremendously happy and highly motivated piano students.

Herb Kelleher is the founder and CEO of Southwest Airlines. In the last twenty years, he has built one of the most profitable airlines in the business. Kelleher has been known to come to company functions dressed as Elvis and sing to his staff. He once settled a legal dispute concerning a marketing slogan by arm wrestling. Even though he lost the match, he won the admiration of his opponent and was granted the rights to continue using the slogan. From time to time, Kelleher can be found serving soda during a flight. For Halloween, he practically closes the entire home office and turns the building into a giant haunted house. Kelleher has been known to join last-minute fishing trips with company employees. This same kind of passion can be seen in his employees. One flight attendant used to hide in the overhead storage bins only to pop out when an unsuspecting passenger boarded and tried to stow baggage. Southwest is not the largest airline but it consistently makes money and earns "Industry Best" awards. Kelleher's passion for his people and company are what have made Southwest the model airline in their industry.

Brooks Robinson was one of the best third baseman to play baseball. He played in the major league for 23 years and participated in four World Series. Brooks holds the record for number of games played at third base, total number of assists, and has the all time best fielding average. In addition, he has been named as an American League Most Valuable Player. After receiving the highest honor a baseball player can earn, being elected to the Hall of Fame, Brooks said, "I'm here because baseball is a passion to me. It was never work."

Passion is contagious. Others will feed off your passion and you off theirs. Passion is putting in 12, 14 or even 16-hour days. Passion is waking up in the middle of the night to make a note of something to do the next day. Passion is the love for success. It is unyielding, ever flowing and always there to call upon.

Performance

Work is love made visible.
- Kahlil Gibran -Syrian born American mystic poet and painter.

Your level of performance may be the difference between success and failure. Someone once said that anything worth doing is worth doing well. The difference between doing a job well and just completing the task may only require a little bit of additional effort. Always ask yourself two questions: "Did I do the best job possible"? and "How could I do a better job?" Good work on the sub-elements of your plan will yield good results on the plan as a whole. *Remember, if you won't settle for less than great effort, you won't have to live with less than great results.*

Persistence

Success seems to be largely a matter of hanging on after others have let go.
- William Feather -Twentieth century novelist known for *The Federalist*.

Success seldom comes overnight. Success takes time. It's not a matter of "if" but rather "when." A study done by *Forbes Magazine* about entrepreneurship revealed that a person's primary desire to have their own business must be so great that even repeated failures don't discourage them. But instead, difficulties and failure rather serve to strengthen their resolve to successfully run their own company. In other words, persistence is the key.

Sally Jessy Raphael was fired 18 times from 24 different jobs. Today her talk show is considered one of the best in broadcasting. If she had given up at any point along the way, she would never have achieved such tremendous results. Sally's setbacks allowed her to refocus and moved her forward to her eventual success.

A little boy named Harland was only six years old when his father died, but it was up to him to take care of his younger brother and sister. At twelve, his stepfather kicked him out of the house. This was the end of Harland's schooling and the beginning of a life filled with hard work. He worked at farming, as a streetcar conductor, and became a private in the Army at 16. Upon discharge, Harland worked at various jobs on the railroad. Still a teenager, Harland was supporting his then-divorced mother, and his younger brother and sister. While working for the railroad, Harland took several correspondence courses. He spent a brief time working as a lawyer, but his legal career was cut short by a fight with a court justice. Harland returned to the railroad once again. He sold insurance and stocks and had a failed lighting business. Harland had experience with failed service stations. He owned a restaurant and motel combination when in 1939 a new interstate highway was built, leaving Harland's business off the beaten path. He was forced to sell off his assets to cover outstanding debts and he was left with his $105.00 per month Social Security to live on. During those years of many failures, Harland had done something else. He had perfected a recipe for fried chicken. At the age of 66, Harland set out to sell the rights to use his fried chicken recipe. In 1964, at the age of 72, Colonel Harland D. Sanders sold his Kentucky Fried Chicken chain of over 600 franchises for two million dollars and a lifetime contract. Many failures and setbacks were overcome on Colonel Sanders' road to success. Today Kentucky Fried Chicken is one of the largest restaurant chains in the world!

You must work on your dream every day. Nourish your ideas and stick with your convictions. You can succeed! Doubters will be all around you, but they do not know or understand the principles of success. Or they may be envious of your commitment and desire to succeed. Only *you* know that you can reach your goals. Your motivation is intrinsic. Keep moving forward.

The experience you have as you work toward your goals can be as rewarding as the goals themselves. Along the way, you will build character and develop discipline. The gains from achieving each goal will make it easier to achieve the next goal. You now have momentum working in your favor. Don't be afraid of the process. The process itself will make each succeeding goal all the more reachable.

As an accomplished marathon runner, I learned several important things. First, I learned to pace myself. I achieved my best results when each mile was consistent in time. If I started out too fast, I faded at the end of the race. However, if I picked a goal pace and maintained it mile after mile, I always finished strong and within my goal time. Second, and perhaps more importantly, I learned to continuously monitor my body as I ran. This allowed me to adjust my stride, my breathing patterns, and my posture. But it also allowed me to be aware of the different stages of stress and comfort my body experienced. These stages alternated between feeling good, to feeling discomfort, to feeling good again. At those times when I felt discomfort, it helped to know that if I kept on going, I would feel good again. These same lessons can be applied to life. When things are not going the way you'd like, keep on moving. Maintain your forward momentum. This stage will pass and success can be around the corner. The race toward your primary goals may be long, but the trophy (success) only goes to those who are patient and endure.

There will be times as you work toward success that

you come up against what appears to be a brick wall. This may be the most significant moment of your journey. ***Don't be the one to give in.*** Someone or something will break. If you are determined not to let it be you, then success will be close at hand.

When I first met my wife, Renee, I was immediately attracted to her. Unfortunately, I did not become one of Renee's primary desires as early as she had become one of mine. I was so persistent that at one point she asked me if I knew the meaning of the word "no." I said that it was not in my dictionary. To back up my statement I copied the page from the dictionary, cut out the word "no," and re-arranged the words to form a full page. Then, I mailed Renee a copy of this page out of "my" dictionary that showed the word "no" was not in it. Persistence helped me achieve my most important primary desire, to marry Renee.

Potential

I've never met a person, I don't care what his condition, in whom I could not see possibilities. I don't care how much a man may consider himself a failure, I believe in him, for he can change the thing that is wrong in his life any time he is ready and prepared to do it. Whenever he develops the desire, he can take away from his life the thing that is defeating it. The capacity for reformation and change lies within.
- Preston Bradley -Twentieth century American author.

Potential for greatness and success is inherent in all human beings. The difference between the outcomes that people achieve is that some people learn the techniques for turning potential into reality. We all have the proper tools. We must recognize these tools and apply them in order to achieve the greatness we desire. Those who do not achieve greatness choose to not achieve it. They do not realize the potential that is already in them and they do not use the tools. Success must be earned. It requires work. Mediocrity will come by default.

A few years ago, a friend of mine had a million-dollar home improvement company, Arrowhead Vinyl

Windows. Chuck was approached with the possibility of a joint venture with a British firm, Spectus uPVC Systems. It required that he negotiate business details with Spectus, obtain local financing, design and obtain tooling for five complete vinyl window systems, and lay out the marketing strategy and produce sales materials for a complete line of new windows. Chuck had to do all of this and keep his original company running. Tooling alone normally takes three to six months per extrusion die, and he needed over twelve dies! But after only eight months, with many sleepless nights and temporary setbacks, the deal was complete. Later Chuck told me: "It's amazing how much you can accomplish if you are totally committed to an idea and completely possessed with making it work." Today the company he started has annual sales of over 17 million dollars!

What you must understand is that the price will be paid either way. You can pay the price of hard work to reach your potential and enjoy your successes, or you can pay the price of lost opportunities and not achieving the things you really want in life. Two commonalities in all human beings are inherent success potential and the decision whether or not to tap that potential. The choice is yours.

Prejudge

When you meet a man, you judge him by his clothes; when you leave, you judge him by his heart.
- Russian Proverb

Don't prejudge!

Some years ago, a customer who was poorly dressed entered our showroom. I talked with the gentleman and wrote up the order for the items he wanted, but I did not do much "selling" or work to increase the order. Actually, I doubted the man would be able to pay for the order, which totaled about one-thousand-dollars. But I was mistaken. When I told the gentleman the total, he reached into his pocket and paid me the one-thousand-dollars in cash, before I had even filled the order. I then realized that I could have easily sold him several hundred dollars more. Had I taken this customer more seriously, had I not pre-judged him, I probably could have increased the order thirty or forty percent.

In the home improvement business it is common for salespeople to "qualify" their leads. This means that if the lead is just for one storm door or one replacement window, the salesperson will call the homeowner to try and determine if it is really worth his time to go out and price the job. Many times, this will just turn off the potential customer and kill the sale. The real champions in the home improvement business know that once they are in the home, they may identify other window problems ultimately with the possibility of a larger sale. It is not uncommon therefore, to turn a "one window" lead into a whole house of windows or windows for the first floor and a patio door.

Sam Walton was the founder of Walmart. Before he died he was the wealthiest man in America; but if you judged Sam Walton's wealth by the car he drove, you would have been badly mistaken. You see, Sam Walton usually drove a pickup truck.

Prejudging can cost you money. Do not decide what the financial capabilities are of others. Looks may be deceiving. Maintain your aggressiveness and always give 100%, no matter what the situation looks like. You may be surprised with the outcome.

Priorities

He who every morning plans the transactions of the day and follows out that plan carries a thread that will guide him through the labyrinth of the most busy life.
- Victor Hugo -Nineteenth century poet, dramatist, and novelist.

There are many excellent scheduling and prioritizing systems on the market today. There is, in fact, a growing awareness of the need for these devices. I encourage you to purchase such a device and the related training tools. A good planning device will help you gain control over your time and increase your efficiency. It will help you move closer to fulfilling your primary desires.

It is important that the planning mechanism you buy be more than just a calendar and a priority list of things to do. You probably have enough of those already. You should have detailed descriptions of your primary desires and outlines of your plans in your planning device. This will enable you to include the elements of those plans in your daily prioritized task list. Getting these important, proactive tasks onto your daily list will enable you to continually work towards your primary desires.

By planning beyond the daily tasks, you will be in a proactive mode. You will be addressing the issues you want and spending your time productively. You will be able to deal with issues before they get out of hand, thus avoiding ending up in a reactive mode and being forced to use crisis management to just keep your head above water. If your entire day is spent prioritizing crises, you will not move forward on your goals. If, instead, you prioritize tasks that are designed to move you towards your primary desires, then you will be highly productive. The last thing anyone needs is another crisis "to do" list. What you do need is a proactive, management activity list, in which the activities lead to the successful completion of a well thought out plan, enabling you to reach your primary desires.

Your time management tool will be a permanent log of all your discussions and conversations. It allows you to retain the pertinent facts from any meeting so that you can recall them when needed.

For example, suppose you meet with a supplier who quotes you a price for raw materials of $75 per thousand and you order 50,000 pieces. When the invoice arrives, however, you are billed at the rate of $80 per thousand. By referring to your planning device you will be able to correct the mistake and save yourself $250.00. If you maintain a daily journal in your time planning device, you will have accurate records of that meeting, including the time, location, and length of the meeting. One person I know even records the daily weather and references it when recalling a meeting with customers. You should see the looks on their faces when he tells someone what the weather was when they had a meeting six weeks prior! They think he has genius level memory when in fact he is just a good note taker and uses his time planning device to his advantage.

Many people try to take care of the "easy" tasks first in the morning. However, the easy tasks are usually the least important. Instead you should prioritize *all* the tasks necessary to reach your goals and then proceed one by one through your list, taking no short cuts! Discipline yourself to stick with the order of your list. By prioritizing your tasks you will get maximum benefits from your efforts. You will be tempted to skip around a tough item to take care of an easy task but resist. If you jump around from task to task you waste time and may end up having to repeat a task. Stick to a well thought out and prioritized list in order to efficiently manage your time.

If your car radiator hadn't been serviced in several years, you would not add anti-freeze and then decide to flush out the radiator. If you did, you would be wasting both your time and money. Instead you would approach the problem logically. This same principle applies to everything you do.

Prioritizing increases your productivity since each step you take, each action you complete, will move you towards the fulfillment of your primary desires (see Productivity). Even if you don't do everything on your list in a given day, if you stick to your list, you will have accomplished the most important items.

Do not let yourself be constantly interrupted. Eliminate spending time on items that disguise themselves as urgent priorities. A ringing phone may seem to be shouting "pick me up." But remember, a phone call might be important but it may also just be a distraction. Consider setting aside time to work on your prioritized list of tasks and don't take calls during that time.

I discovered that my team of factory employees could produce more in four 10-hour days than in five 8-hour days because they didn't have to start and stop as many times. Each time they started up, the workers had to figure out where they were in the work cycle and they had to let the machinery warm up. After any interruption, you will have to regroup your thoughts before proceeding. This ends up being wasted time. Be aware of interruptions and eliminate them whenever possible.

There are two ways of getting tasks done. You can do them yourself or you can delegate them to someone else. Delegating work is a valuable way of increasing the amount of work you can accomplish. You should, however, be sure that you delegate to a competent individual. By combining your efforts with the efforts of qualified assistants, you will be able to expand your coverage.

A person's shadow will extend a specific distance on the ground. If someone stood at the end of your shadow then his/her shadow would add to the length of yours. If another person stood at the end of the second person's shadow then his/her shadow would extend even further. By adding competent people to your team the amount of ground your shadow covers will grow and the amount of work you do and the tasks you accomplish will increase dramatically.

Carefully prioritize your tasks. Stay with your prioritized task list throughout the day. Whenever possible, delegate and review work in order to cover as much ground as possible. By carefully managing your time, you achieve more.

Problems

Difficulties are meant to rouse, not discourage. The human spirit is to grow strong by conflict.
- William Ellery Channing -Nineteenth century American religious leader.

Problems are an inevitable part of reality. Some people are so afraid of problems that they suffer increased stress and are unable to act rationally or logically. Actually, challenges force you to deal with tough situations and make hard decisions. This is when your resources are tested, your character is stretched, and you have the opportunity to grow. As you handle more challenges, your abilities will expand. Fortunately, every challenge leads to increased knowledge, whether or not you are successful dealing with the problem. You can learn from your mistakes just as well as from your successes.

All successful people know that problems and challenges will arise. Some can be anticipated; some cannot. Regardless, know that you will face challenges and that you have the ability to solve them. Most experts agree that the solutions for problems are built into the problems themselves. By understanding that you will face tough times, you will be able to react calmly when they do arise. This will enable you to make better decisions.

A good way to deal with a problem is to write it down. Once it is on paper, you can see the problem more clearly and look at it more objectively. You will be able to distance yourself emotionally from the situation. Now, you can decide if you really have a problem and, if so, how much importance to give it. It may be easier to work on several smaller problems than on one large one, so if possible, break the problem into parts that you can attack separately. Check with your mentor or support group. Find out if anyone has dealt with a similar problem before. Write down the best possible solutions based on your experiences and on the advice of the accomplished people around you.

When handled quickly and effectively, problems create opportunities. Take advantage of these opportunities, then continue with your plans.

Procrastination

Even if you're on the right track-you'll get run over if you just sit there.
- Arthur Godfrey -Radio and television personality.

Procrastination is a bad habit. It is the destroyer of goals and dreams and achievement. If you procrastinate you should look to replace the habit of procrastination with the habit of action (see Habit). A good slogan to remember is "You can't be great if you procrastinate."

The best day to start a project is today. In school, students often put off until the last minute writing a report or doing an assignment. Finally, when the fear of failure outweighs the discomfort of having to do the report, they are motivated to start and find that the project really isn't that bad. Sometimes they realize that if they only had started earlier, they would have had more time and might have done a better job. Then, they swear that *next time* they will start the day the assignment is given and get it done earlier. But, next time they fall into the same procrastination trap.

People procrastinate because they pay closer attention to the comfort of the moment than to long term pleasure and long lasting satisfaction. For example, it would have been much more comfortable on those cold, windy mornings to stay in bed rather than to get out and run. However, it would have been impossible to achieve my long term goals of running the Boston Marathon if I hadn't exercised diligently each morning. The long term satisfaction of accomplishing my goal outweighed any short term pain or discomfort of early morning training. When I did, in fact, qualify for and subsequently run the Boston Marathon, all the work and sacrifice was more than worth it!

Remember, your mind can only focus on one concept at a time. To move from a life of procrastination to one of immediate action you must shift your focus from the pain of the immediate action to the pleasure of the eventual outcome. By placing our attention and emphasis on the pleasure to be derived, you will be motivated to move forward with your project. The anticipated pleasure will generate the passion, energy and commitment necessary to complete your project and achieve your primary desires.

As soon as you identify a project, take some action, no matter how small, to begin the project. A project is much easier to complete, once it has been started, even if the first step is small. If the task is large or complex, break it down into several smaller projects that will be easier to tackle.

Establish deadlines for each part of the project. Make it a game. If you finish a project before a deadline, reward yourself. As you begin, you may start slowly and with small steps. But as you move forward, you will pick up momentum.

If "any job worth doing is worth doing well," then any goal worth having is worth pursuing *now*! Procrastinating only creates "negative momentum" (see Momentum) and actually pushes you further away from the achievement of your primary desires. You can either move forward or slip backwards. Which direction are **you** moving? What are your primary desires? Make a small start today!

Productivity

It is more than probable that the average man could, with no injury to his health, increase his efficiency fifty percent.
- Sir Walter Scott -Nineteenth century British writer of ballads and novels.

Being productive is paramount to achieving your goals. Ask yourself, "**Does this activity move me closer to achieving my primary desires**?" If it does, then you are being productive. If it doesn't, then your time is not being well spent.

Once your goals are outlined and you have formed a plan to reach those goals, you must do those things that will fulfill the elements of your plan. The average person wastes a great deal of time each day. Think about it. How efficient do you work? Do you combine tasks to save time? For example, do you run several errands at once or do you make separate trips away from your desk?

Activity increases productivity. And a great way to increase activity is to do more than one thing at a time. For example, you can listen to motivational and educational tapes when you are driving your car or getting dressed in the morning. Instead of eating lunch alone, eat with a client, or mentor, or someone else you can learn from. Be creative.

In order to evaluate your level of productivity, analyze a typical work day. Write down everything you do and the amount of time you spend doing it. At the end of the day, determine what percentage of your work day was spent on unproductive tasks. Could you generate forty-five extra productive minutes a day? In a year's time, that would be equivalent to having one whole extra month. Imagine what you could accomplish if you dedicated a whole month to one project! One month represents 8.3% of your total annual income. How much extra income could you earn? What if you could generate an extra ninety minutes a day?

Remember your primary desires. At times they may be in contradiction to one-another. What is productive for one goal may not be productive for another. Balance and temporary imbalance should be considered when evaluating your productivity.

Reality

Reality isn't the way you wish things to be, nor the way they appear to be, but the way they actually are.
- Robert J. Ringer -Businessman and author.

It is not realistic to expect you can go through life thinking positively **all** of the time. Surely you will encounter negative events that will require your attention. There will be moments of concern or even self-doubt. The key is to realize that these moments are fleeting. Don't let them build momentum and distract you from applying time proven techniques for dealing with the challenges of life.

Deal with the truth. Recognize the existing situation for what it is and properly assess your opportunities and potentials. For example, although I love basketball I know that I will never play it professionally. I am too short and can't jump high enough. I am realistic enough to know that those facts are not going to change no matter what I do. Likewise, if you are broke, then you are broke. It doesn't help to sugar coat that fact. What you can do is address the issue, set goals, and come up with a plan to change the situation. The fact that you are broke now may be a reality. But remember, it is also a reality that, through change, hard work and dedication, the future can and will be different from the present.

Regroup

Men are anxious to improve their circumstances, but are unwilling to improve themselves; they therefore remain bound.
- James Allen -Nineteenth century American novelist.

In every journey, there are setbacks. When setbacks occur it is important not to lose sight of your destination (goals). You can learn from your mistakes. Non-achievers become negative and withdraw when they encounter setbacks. Achievers learn from their mistakes, store the information, and then use energy and creativity to correct the situation and move forward. Remember, it is not the single battle but the *war* we want to win.

Champions have the ability to regroup after setbacks. They know that they haven't failed until they quit. They use feedback to evaluate current plans and make changes where necessary. Maintaining focus on your primary desires and the resulting goals is the key to being able to regroup after setbacks. Since we know that we can only process one thought at a time, focusing on a poor performance will prevent you from evaluating and redirecting your energy to achieve positive results.

After any setback, ask yourself, "What do I need to do to regroup and move toward success?" By asking yourself this question, you will put your creative mind to work on positive solutions, not on negative events. Developing the ability to regroup will help you overcome setbacks and enable you to achieve.

Responsibility

Make up your mind to act decidedly and take the consequences. No good is ever done in this world by hesitation.
- Thomas Henry Huxley -Nineteenth century British biologist.

First, you are responsible to yourself. You deserve and have a right to success and happiness. You owe that to yourself and you have the power to deliver.

Second, you are responsible to others. The people around you deserve the very best you can give them. They believe in you and support you with energy, enthusiasm, love, and commitment.

In 1993, the mid-west United States endured the worst flood on record since the discovery of the "new world." As flood waters rose, thousands of people from all over the country descended on St. Louis and other affected areas to help with the sandbagging project. While my son Geoffrey and I were helping fill sandbags one afternoon, I was amazed by the number of volunteers. People who were not even affected by the flood turned out to do whatever they could to help those in need. During the weeks of volunteer work, friendships were made, business was transacted, and even romances begun. People came to give of themselves but left with more than they ever imagined. By showing a responsibility to others, everyone came out ahead.

If you are responsible to others, they, in turn, will be responsible to you. Think about it. If you provide enough other people with what they are looking for, they will provide you with what you are looking for (see Give).

Scale

Obviously, the highest type of efficiency is that which can utilize existing material to the best advantage.
- Jawaharlal Nehru -First prime minister of independent India.

The scale of projects may change, but the same rules and concepts hold true whether you are a 7-year old child wanting a pack of bubble gum or a 25-year old newlywed seeking your first house. There is something you desire and you may or may not have the means to afford it. The Success Model will help you in either of these cases.

Many people spend valuable time working toward small goals when they could use the same techniques to reach goals of much larger scale.

A (shoe) salesperson who works for small commissions will have low earnings. A person selling products that pay larger commissions is in a position to have much greater earnings. Both salespeople must work hard and both must be successful using similar skills; but only one of the salespeople has the greater opportunity. He is working on a larger scale.

If you are going to work hard for something, make it worth your while. It may not take any more effort or time to catch a big fish than a small one.

Self-Image

They can conquer who believe they can.
- John Dryden -Seventeenth century British author.

Being satisfied with yourself is critical to a good self-image. If you have good feelings about yourself, you are more likely to treat others around you the way they should be treated. This applies to family members, customers, co-workers and employees. You are most apt to get the response you desire, if you treat others the way they deserve and want to be treated.

Your self-image limits or enhances your ability to achieve. If you look at yourself as a loser, it is impossible to be a winner. If you have a good, healthy self-image, you will have a greater will and ability to succeed. Development of a good image, is critical to the successful application of the other key words defined in this book.

People with a good self-image see their optimal selves and their actual selves as almost the same. A recent Gallup Poll revealed that people with high self-esteem were happier, more productive, and healthier than their counter-parts without it.

If you don't see yourself worthy of your primary desires, then you won't let yourself achieve them. Both my neighbor and I sent our sons for personal training so they could develop their skills to play Little League. We sent them to different coaches, both of whom had played professional ball. My son's coach charged $7.50 an hour. The other coach charged $30.00 an hour. Both boys received approximately the same level of training. The difference was that the other coach had a much higher image of his self-worth. He believed he was worth $30.00 an hour and that's what he charged. Estimating that each coach worked with just three children a week, the difference between their annual earnings for this part-time job was thirty five hundred dollars. Invested over a twenty-year period the difference would be two-hundred-thousand-dollars!

Many people have restricted their self-image to a point where they don't realize they are worthy of tremendous success. Breaking down these walls will open your horizons and allow you to freely work toward your primary desires, no matter how great they may seem. We are all worthy of the greatest success.

I have a friend who is starting into the sales training business. His goal is to be able to charge ten-thousand-dollars per day for his sales training seminars. He has a high level of self-worth. He believes he can add more than ten-thousand-dollars value to a client's business. Does he have a right to ask for that kind of money? Sure, he does! And if he can bring that kind of return to a company, it makes good sense. He has the high self-image and high self-worth that will allow him to ask for that fee. Others may ask for less. But he believes and knows in his heart that he is worth every penny of that ten-thousand-dollars.

Some retail companies sell replacement windows to homeowners for $400.00 each. Others sell them for $500.00 or even $650.00. I know one retailer who sells the same basic window for $1,000.00 that others sell for $500.00! Now that's high self-worth and the retailer has the ability to project that high self-worth to others. To do this, you have to believe in the quality of service and product you offer and deliver what you promise. You must show how you feel, not only in how you talk and what you say, but also in how you dress and your overall presentation. Then you will have put yourself in a position where others will believe it.

Our self-image is shaped by the environment in which we grew up. Parents, grandparents and siblings effect our self-image. Successful people realize that their self-image governs their success and work to *reshape* that image. Self-image can be controlled and developed through *self talk*, or self-programming. Your mind cannot distinguish between an actual successful experience and a vividly imagined one. Since we develop our self-image based on events and beliefs, it is important to program your mind with the facts and thoughts that *you want*. Successful people learn very early to control their thoughts. You cannot achieve positive results with negative thoughts, and you will not achieve negative results with positive thoughts. Athletes practice an important event in their mind, rehearsing each step in advance so that when it is time for the actual performance, their mind perceives this as just a repetition of a previously successful experience. Prepare for a variety of different circumstances. Then, if and when that situation arises, you won't have to make decisions, you will just act.

You can pre-program yourself for specific events or beliefs.

Read the following statements out loud.

- I control my destiny.
- I am glad I am me.
- No opinion of me is more important than my own.
- My conversations with myself are important.
- I don't need the approval of others, I need my own approval.
- I know what is right and what is wrong.
- I am successful because I study success and work at it.
- I will achieve because the ability to achieve is already inside me.

After reading those statements how do you feel? you should feel great. These affirmations are designed to infuse you with confidence, to remind you that inside you is a kernel of self-worth and red corpuscled energy that will project you beyond the nay-sayers in your environment.

By utilizing self-talk, you can program yourself for success and at the same time create the self-belief necessary to start towards your most valued goals. But this is not enough. **All the affirmations in the world won't do you any good if you don't take action!** Action is still the basis for getting results.

You should feel worthy of success. You would not have success, if you didn't deserve it. Your self-image must grow and expand to allow you to be comfortable and happy with the successes you are seeking. If you are not prepared for success, when it comes, you will not be able to hold onto it. Many people who have earned millions of dollars or had large inheritances lost their fortunes because they were not ready to deal with their success.

Self-confidence is an important part of your self-image. Self-confidence comes from increased knowledge and proven success of a job well done. Self-confidence will come from overall preparedness, which is a result of study, acquired knowledge through experiences, and discussions with your mentor. Self-confidence is an instantaneous gratification of the results of your efforts to educate yourself.

Write your own positive affirmations. Repeat them daily. Read and listen to both educational and motivational material. Prepare your mind and self-image for the successes you will be achieving.

Serve

He is great who confers the most benefits.
- Ralph Waldo Emerson

Your ability to accomplish what you set out to achieve is directly related to your ability to serve others. We all like to be served. In a restaurant, when a waiter gives good service he usually gets a good tip. If he provides poor or mediocre service he may get a small tip. No matter what field you are in, your level of achievement is dependent on your level of service.

The natural law of reciprocity requires that you give something first before you have the right to ask for something. By first presenting a "gift" to your customer, friend, co-worker, or family member, you are putting them in a position of wanting to reciprocate your generosity. When you give someone else what they need, they will give you what you need in return.

In order to best serve other people, you have to know what it is they need and want. You can learn a great deal about people by being alert, through good listening techniques (see Listen), and through research. Serve as many people as you can and you will see a high return on your efforts.

Skills

Few things are impossible to diligence and skill.
- Samuel Johnson -Eighteenth century British writer and lexicographer.

This section refers to the specific skills necessary to successfully implement your written plans. Once the goals are established, the plans written and you are ready to proceed on your mission, you must stop and take stock of your skills. Your skill level will play a big part in your success. Your current skill level is not as important as knowing what skill level you need and how you are going to reach that level.

Reading this book indicates that you have already decided you want to be a success and you want to develop success skills. You may need people skills, or communication skills, or money management skills. Figure out what skills you need and then decide how to go about getting them. You can learn through books, school, video and audiotape recordings, attend lectures, and private discussions (be careful from whom you take advice). Working for someone else is a great way to learn. While skills are *specific*, knowledge is general and balanced. Both are important.

Developing your skills will allow you to successfully implement your plan. Your level of frustration will be inversely related to your skill level. As your skills grow you will be able to effectively handle an increasing amount of situations and get the results you seek.

Truths

The fundamental laws are in the long run merely statements that every event is itself and not some different event.
- C.S. Lewis -Nineteenth century British writer and critic.

Natural laws or truths are things that we cannot change. They affect everyone the same way. They affect our lives and our quest for achievement.

Sir Isaac Newton recognized the natural law of gravity: "What goes up must come down." This knowledge makes it possible to determine what will and won't happen in any given situation with respect to gravity. An engineer who didn't know the law of gravity, who didn't know that water will always run downhill, could not accurately plan an irrigation system. Knowing the rules that affect his field of interest is crucial to his success.

What rules do you need to know? What are the unwritten laws and fundamentals that will assist you. Seek the advice of your mentor. You may not even know a rule exists unless someone tells you.

It is much easier to play the game if you know the rules. And it is impossible to win the game unless you know the rules. Playing by the rules maximizes your efforts to work within the system.

Visualization

The greatest discovery of my generation is that human beings can alter their lives by altering their attitudes of mind.
- William James -Nineteenth century psychologist and philosopher.

It is important to be able to see the big picture; to see what you want; to see yourself achieving your goals. If you can't see the target how can you hit it? This is called being *vision-driven*.

You must see the destination before you start the journey. I laid out the cover photo for this book before I wrote the first page. I thought of the cover and pictured the book in my mind, even before I began writing. When you clearly see what it is you are seeking, you can logically make the plans to reach your goals.

Imagine yourself at a target range. If you see the target well and practice good marksmanship, you will hit the bullseye every time. However, if you have poor vision and have forgotten your glasses, you will not hit the target, no matter how good a marksman you are. To be able to hit a target you must have good, clear vision. You have to be able to see your goal (target) with high definition in order to hit it! It's impossible to hit the bullseye, unless your vision is clear. Make the decision to hit the bullseye, every time!

A friend of mine wrote and self-published a book on parent-teenager communications. She realized that if her book was going to sell, she would have to be the one to promote it. Her goal was to get on The Donahue Show. That was some goal! She felt that that kind of national exposure would make her book a big success. She was so convinced she could get on Donahue that she bought a dress to wear on the show. This dress, her "Donahue Dress," hung in her closet as a constant reminder of what she wanted. After much work and countless setbacks, Yvonne had several articles written about her book. She appeared on The Today Show, Good Morning America, Oprah, Sally Jessy Raphael and, eventually, The Phil Donahue Show. Her hard work and vision paid off. She sold over 20,000 copies of her book. This success led to a publishing contract with a major publishing house and eventual sales of over 100,000 books!

Visualization is a key motivator to keep you on track. In order to accomplish what you need to on a daily basis, it is imperative to maintain a high energy level. In order to create this energy (passion), every morning when you get up, visualize your goals and what it will be like when you achieve them. Close your eyes and see what it is you desire and how your life will be better when you achieve your goals. Each day see yourself a little bit closer to achieving your goals. The excitement you generate will get your day off to a positive and dynamic start.

You

No one but you is withholding your own from you.
- Thomas Bland -British author.

It all begins with you! I once heard a saying, "Pray as if God determines everything, act as if *you* determine everything."

When my son Geoffrey was first playing Little League, he was so worried about striking out that he would not swing at the ball. He would either get a walk or get called out on strikes. Although I tried several times to explain that he needed to swing at the ball, I just couldn't convince him to try. One day we went to the batting cages to practice, and much to my amazement, Geoffrey hit almost every pitch! When the machine was about to throw the last ball, I told him: "No matter what, do not swing." After the ball passed him, I asked: "Why weren't you able to hit that ball?" His sister Sara quickly responded: "Because he didn't swing at it, Daddy." It was as if a light came on in Geoffrey's head. He smiled from ear-to-ear. From that day on, he swung at everything he could reach and was able to get many hits.

Geoffrey learned what you already know: It takes action to get a reaction. You control whether you will act and how you will act. You control your destiny. We are all born with the latent ability to be successful. It is up to *you* to apply The Success Model in your life.

The Bottom Line

When I first saw Pablo Picasso's simple painting "Daisies," I said to myself, "I could have done that." But the point is I did not have the idea for the painting. Picasso did. If you understand and implement the terms discussed in this book, you can paint the priceless picture of the subject of *your* choice. Your picture may be your job, your hobby, or your life.

The Time Value of Money is a well known and taught concept. But there is no money value to time. Once time is gone it can never be regained. All the money in the world can't buy you any more time. Make the best use of your time *today*. Maintain balance in your life. Do what is necessary to live a balanced life and achieve your primary desires.

The promise of the future is a tremendous power that drives people to set goals and achieve great things. If you vividly paint the promise of the future, you can *borrow* the impact of that promise to affect your actions today. Use this promise, and what it holds for you and those you love, to drive you to dedicate yourself to success. If the promise of the future is great enough, then you will be willing to pay the price to achieve success. The reward at the end of the journey must be greater than the price you have to pay. You must see the benefits and rewards of your goal so vividly, and desire the results so fervently, that you are willing to pay the price.

Learn the words taught in this book. Apply them to your life. We all have greatness inside of us. The successful people of this world are the ones that bring it to the surface. I can not make you great. I can only share my philosophies with you on how to attain the greatness that is within us all. If you believe in these ideas and apply them, you, too, will be great and it will be you who achieved this greatness. It is you who is responsible for your successes.

There are two final steps that you must take to insure your outcome on the road to success.

1. Commit yourself to applying The Success Model for three weeks.

2. Within 24 hours after finishing this book, teach The Success Model to at least two other people.

By committing three weeks to the model, you will apply the time necessary for these techniques to become *learned habits*. Twenty-one days of practice will translate into sustained commitment.

Teaching The Success Model will help you better understand and internalize the principles discussed here. And sharing the principles with others will make you more responsible for them. You will, in effect, reinforce your commitment to the Model. By teaching the Model to others, you will have objectively announced your intent to follow the system. Then, your subconscious will push you forward to fulfill that commitment.

If you want to reach your goal, it has to be within your capability. You must live in the present and not dwell on past failures. Most important, keep your eye on your goal and keep aiming at what you are trying to achieve. Do not let anything get in the way of your success. It is your responsibility and destiny to find *the best* that is within *you*. This best is *your success*. It is reachable. It is attainable. It is an obligation to yourself and those around you to achieve it. Shakespeare said, "The future is the undiscovered country." What lies ahead in your undiscovered country?

Some people believe that we were all put on this earth with a specific mission such as being a doctor, a teacher, or a parent. I believe, however, that our mission is to find out what it is we really want, what our primary desires are, what we are willing to "walk through fire for." As we discover what our mission is, we will generate the positive feelings and excitement that allow us to take our primary desires through The Success Model. No one wants to walk down the road of life; you want to sprint along working on your primary desires with the full conviction and force that The Success Model gives.

This book has sought to break down into simplistic terms the concepts you need to understand and implement in your life to guarantee success. These are simple concepts, but it takes dedication and commitment to get results. The application of these concepts takes effort, but you can do it.

A story is told of an old man long ago who has a dream about great treasure that is buried by the palace clock tower in the capital city, far away. When the man awakens he dismisses the dream and goes about his business. The man has the dream a second time, but again he dismisses it as only a dream. A third night the old man has the same dream of a treasure by the clock tower next to the palace in the far away capital city. The next morning the man feels compelled to travel to the capital. He sets out walking, traveling many days, sleeping under trees and in barns. Upon arriving in the capital he goes to the palace clock tower but finds many guards nearby. Not wanting to attract attention, he leaves but returns each morning for the next ten days to look around. One morning the captain of the palace guard asks the old man why he has been visiting the clock tower every day. The old man tells the guard his dream about the hidden treasure. The guard began to laugh and says that such dreams were nonsense. The guard tells the old man that he had had a similar dream and that if he traveled to a village far, far, away and dug under the bed of an old man he would find a great treasure. With that, the old man thanks the guard, departs and makes the long, hard trip back home. When he arrives, he begins digging under his bed, until he discovers a treasure. The moral of the story: Sometimes you have to travel far to find a treasure that is near.

You have traveled far to get where you are today and you will travel far as you seek the education, knowledge, mentors, and skills necessary to write and implement the plans necessary to achieve your primary desires. But the treasure is near. The ability to achieve is in us all. With The Success Model you can unleash it. Direct it. Focus it on your primary desires and you, too, will enjoy a life of complete and balanced success. *What would your life be like if you achieved all your primary desires?*

Summary of Quotes

All human activity is prompted by desire.
- Bertrand Russel

Keep changing. When you're through changing, you're through.
- Francis Bacon

Successful generals make plans to fit circumstances, but do not try to create circumstances to fit plans.
- General George S. Patton, Jr.

Few men are lacking in capacity, but they fail because they are lacking in application.
- Calvin Coolidge

I want to be all that I am capable of becoming.
- Katherine Mansfield

Any fact facing us is not as important as our attitude toward it, for that determines our success or failure.
- Norman Vincent Peale

Do you want my one-word secret of happiness? It's growth - mental, financial, you name it.
- Harold S. Geneen

Your belief that you can do the thing gives your thought forces their power.
- Robert Collier

The person who makes a success of living is the one who sees his goal steadily and aims for it unswervingly. That is dedication.
- Cecil B. De Mille

Ideas are the root of creation.
- Ernest Dimnet

Crises refine life. In them you discover what you are.
- Allan K. Chalmers

You never will be the person you can be if pressure, tension, and discipline are taken out of your life.
- James G. Bilkey

Every great and commanding movement in the annals of the world is the triumph of enthusiasm. Nothing great was ever achieved without it.
- Ralph Waldo Emerson

Few enterprises of great labor or hazard would be undertaken if we had not the power of magnifying the advantages we expect from them.
- Samuel Johnson

He's no failure. He's not dead yet.
- William Lloyd George

Faith is to believe what we do not see; and the reward of this faith is to see what we believe.
- St. Augustine

He who fears being conquered is sure of defeat.
- Napoleon Bonaparte

He who stops being better stops being good.
- Oliver Cromwell

Consider the postage stamp: its usefulness consists in the ability to stick to one thing till it gets there.
- Josh Billings

If you would be remembered, do one thing superbly well.
- Saunders Norvell

The more he cast away the more he had.
- John Bunyan

People with goals succeed because they know where they are going.
- Earl Nightingale

People seldom improve when they have no other model but themselves to copy after.
- Oliver Goldsmith

Sow an act and you reap a habit.
Sow a habit and you reap a character.
Sow a character and you reap a destiny.
- Charles Reade

Work is the meat of life, pleasure the dessert.
- Bertie Charles Forbes

A single lie destroys a whole reputation of integrity.
- Baltasar Gracian

You are today where your thoughts have brought you; you will be tomorrow where your thoughts take you.
- James Allen

If a man empties his purse into his head, no man can take it away from him. An investment in knowledge always pays the best interest.
- Benjamin Franklin

The final test of a leader is that he leaves behind him in other men the conviction and the will to carry on.
- Walter Lippmann

I think that, as life is action and passion, it is required of a man that he should share the passion and action of his time at peril of being judged not to have lived.
- Oliver Wendell Holmes

If I listen, I have the advantage; if I speak, others have it.
- From the Arabic

Order and simplification are the first steps toward the mastery of a subject...
- Thomas Mann

Chance favors the prepared mind.
- Louis Pasteur

No man is so foolish but he may sometimes give another good counsel, and no man so wise that he may not easily err if he takes no other counsel than his own. He that is taught only by himself has a fool for a master.
- Ben Jonson

Give yourself something to work toward - constantly.
- Mary Kay Ash

As long as I have a want, I have a reason for living. Satisfaction is death.
- George Bernard Shaw

Every body continues in its state of rest, or of uniform motion in a right line, unless it is compelled to change that state by forces impressed upon it.
- Sir Isaac Newton

To be always intending to live a new life, but never find time to set about it-this is as if a man should put off eating and drinking from one day to another till he be starved and destroyed.
- Sir Walter Scott

Let us not be content to wait and see what will happen, but give us the determination to make the right things happen.
- Peter Marshall

Do not wait for extraordinary circumstances to do good; try to use ordinary situations.
- Jean Paul Richter

Never, never rest contented with any circle of ideas, but always be certain that a wider one is still possible.
- Richard Jefferies

A strong passion for any object will ensure success, for the desire of the end will point out the means.
- William Hazlitt

Work is love made visible.
- Kahlil Gibran

Success seems to be largely a matter of hanging on after others have let go.
- William Feather

I've never met a person, I don't care what his condition, in whom I could not see possibilities. I don't care how much a man may consider himself a failure, I believe in him, for he can change the thing that is wrong in his life any time he is ready and prepared to do it. Whenever he develops the desire, he can take away from his life the thing that is defeating it. The capacity for reformation and change lies within.
- Preston Bradley

When you meet a man, you judge him by his clothes; when you leave, you judge him by his heart.
- Russian Proverb

He who every morning plans the transactions of the day and follows out that plan carries a thread that will guide him through the labyrinth of the most busy life.
- Victor Hugo

Difficulties are meant to rouse, not discourage. The human spirit is to grow strong by conflict.
- William Ellery Channing

Even if you're on the right track-you'll get run over if you just sit there.
- Arthur Godfrey

It is more than probable that the average man could, with no injury to his health, increase his efficiency fifty percent.
- Walter Scott

Reality isn't the way you wish things to be, nor the way they appear to be, but the way they actually are.
- Robert J. Ringer

Men are anxious to improve their circumstances, but are unwilling to improve themselves; they therefore remain bound.
- James Allen

Make up your mind to act decidedly and take the consequences. No good is ever done in this world by hesitation.
- Thomas Henry Huxley

Obviously, the highest type of efficiency is that which can utilize existing material to the best advantage.
- Jawaharlal Nehru

They can conquer who believe they can.
- John Dryden

He is great who confers the most benefits.
- Ralph Waldo Emerson

Few things are impossible to diligence and skill.
- Samuel Johnson

The fundamental laws are in the long run merely statements that every event is itself and not some different event.
- C.S. Lewis

No one but you is withholding your own from you.
- Thomas Bland

The greatest discovery of my generation is that human beings can alter their lives by altering their attitudes of mind.
- William James

Index

About The Author

Sam Silverstein earned his Bachelor of Business Administration at the University of Georgia and his Masters in Business Administration from Washington University. He has successfully built a multi-million dollar manufacturing and distribution company and has over 20 years of sales experience. Mr. Silverstein is a member of the National Speakers Association. As president of Sam Silverstein Enterprises, Inc., Mr. Silverstein consults with and speaks to corporations and groups on personal productivity, and teaches his productivity and achievement techniques at public seminars.

Additionally, Mr. Silverstein is active in civic organizations and is an avid marathoner. He and his wife, Renee, have four children and live in a suburb of St. Louis.

For More Information

on how to implement THE SUCCESS MODEL in your organization and on Sam Silverstein training seminars, audio cassette albums, books and consulting services, call or write:

SAM SILVERSTEIN ENTERPRISES, INC.
121 Bellington Suite 400
St. Louis, Missouri 63141
314•878•9252